5507 4669

ENTREPRENEURSHIP

CREATE YOUR OWN BUSINESS

WITH **25** PROJECTS

BUILD IT YOURSELF SERIES

Alex Kahan

Illustrated by Mike Crosier

~ Latest titles in the *Build It Yourself* Series ~

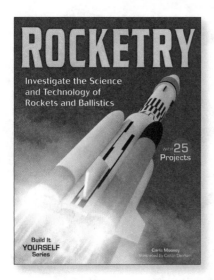
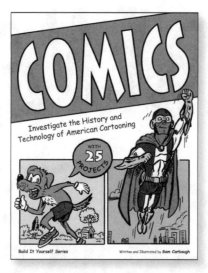

Check out more titles at www.nomadpress.net

Nomad Press
A division of Nomad Communications
10 9 8 7 6 5 4 3 2 1

This book was manufactured by TC Transcontinental Printing,
Beauceville, Québec, Canada
November 2014, Job #67328

ISBN Softcover: 978-1-61930-265-5
ISBN Hardcover: 978-1-61930-284-6

Illustrations by Mike Crosier
Educational Consultant, Marla Conn

Questions regarding the ordering of this book should be addressed to
Nomad Press
2456 Christian St.
White River Junction, VT 05001
www.nomadpress.net

Printed in Canada.

CONTENTS

Interested in Primary Sources?

Look for this icon.

PS

You can use a smartphone or tablet app to scan the QR code and explore more about entrepreneurship! If you don't have a QR code scanning device, there is a list of each url in the Resources on page 120.

Timeline

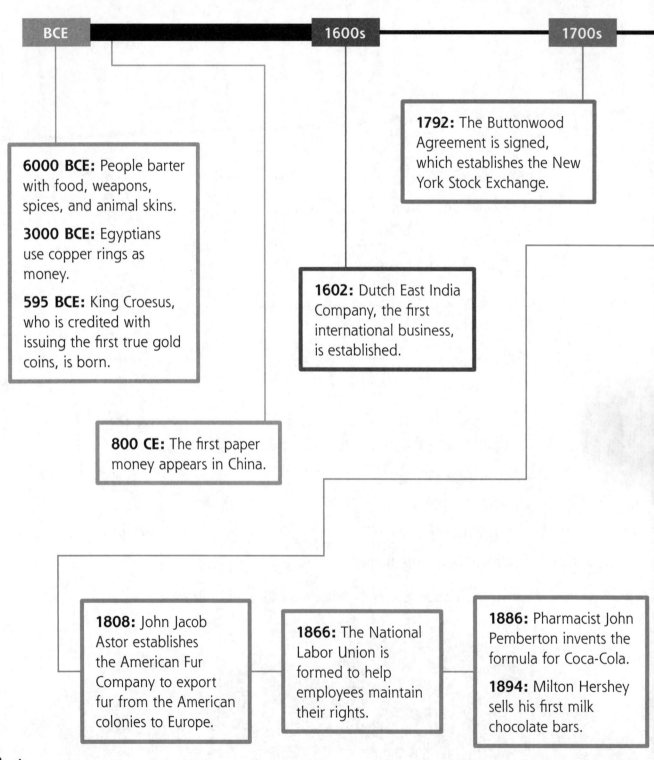

BCE   **1600s**   **1700s**

1792: The Buttonwood Agreement is signed, which establishes the New York Stock Exchange.

6000 BCE: People barter with food, weapons, spices, and animal skins.

3000 BCE: Egyptians use copper rings as money.

595 BCE: King Croesus, who is credited with issuing the first true gold coins, is born.

1602: Dutch East India Company, the first international business, is established.

800 CE: The first paper money appears in China.

1808: John Jacob Astor establishes the American Fur Company to export fur from the American colonies to Europe.

1866: The National Labor Union is formed to help employees maintain their rights.

1886: Pharmacist John Pemberton invents the formula for Coca-Cola.

1894: Milton Hershey sells his first milk chocolate bars.

Timeline

1800s — **1900s** — **2000s**

1906: Will Keith Kellogg establishes the Battle Creek Toasted Corn Flake Company.

1908: Harvard Graduate School of Business is founded.

1913: Henry Ford uses an assembly line to build cars that almost everyone in the United States can afford to buy.

2004: Social media service Facebook launches, created by a college student named Mark Zuckerberg. By 2014, Facebook hosts more than 1.28 billion users.

2008: Robert Croak lives in his office because his company is selling more than a million packs of colorful elastic bracelets called Silly Bandz every week.

2014: GoPro, which Nick Woodman started in 2004 with money saved by selling necklaces out of his van, raises $427 million on its first day as a publicly traded company.

1929: The U.S. economy crashes and the Great Depression starts.

1939: The first commercial television broadcast airs on April 20.

1962: Sam Walton opens Walmart, which grows to be the largest retailer in the world.

1976: Steve Jobs and Steve Wozniak form Apple Computer.

1948: Television reaches a major milestone—1 million people own televisions.

1948: Richard and Maurice McDonald open their first fast-food restaurant.

1985: Nike hires basketball star Michael Jordan to promote its sneakers.

1958: Bank of America issues the first credit card.

1995: Jeff Bezos establishes Amazon, which at the time sells only books over the Internet.

v

Introduction

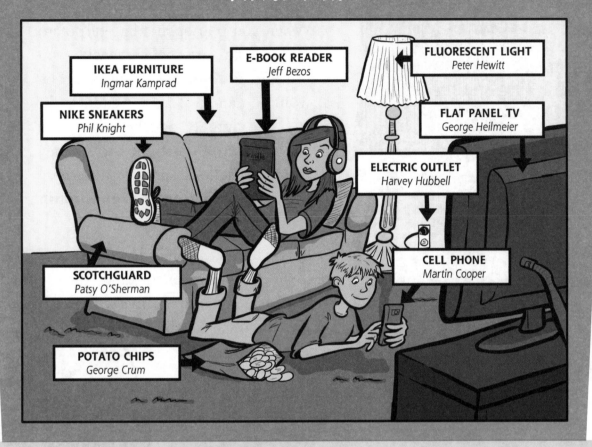

Take a look around you. What kind of shoes are you wearing? Do you have an iPod? The shoes on your feet, the clothes you're wearing, the book or tablet you're reading, the music you listen to, the car your family drives—someone with an idea created a **business** to make each of these things. That person is called an **entrepreneur**.

Entrepreneurs are part of our daily lives. When you walk into a room and turn on the light, you are using something that was **invented** by one of America's earliest entrepreneurs: Thomas Edison.

Words 2 Know!

business: the act of making, buying, or selling goods or services in exchange for money.

entrepreneur: a person who takes a **risk** to start and operate a business.

risk: the chance that something bad will happen.

invent: to be the first to think of or make something new.

technology: tools, methods, and systems used to solve a problem or do work.

innovation: a new invention or way of doing something.

entrepreneurship: taking a risk to start a new business.

social entrepreneur: an entrepreneur who identifies and works to solve social problems to bring about sweeping, long-term change.

industry: the large-scale production of something.

founder: the person who starts a business.

Words 2 Know!

When you pop open a bag of potato chips for an afternoon snack, you are using **technology** developed by a woman named Laura Scudder. In 1926, she figured out how to store potato chips in an airtight bag so they wouldn't go stale. Examples like these of **innovation** and **entrepreneurship** are all around us.

In this book, you'll learn how to become an entrepreneur and turn a great idea into a business. Who knows? Maybe you'll create the next Facebook application or Apple computer!

Why become an entrepreneur? There are many reasons. Maybe you have a great idea and want to share it with others. Maybe you dream of making millions of dollars and becoming famous. Some people become entrepreneurs because they love the idea of working for themselves. Others start their own businesses because they want to help people in need. These people are called **social entrepreneurs**.

Savvy Source

"Social entrepreneurs are not content just to give a fish or teach how to fish. They will not rest until they have revolutionized the fishing **industry**."

—Bill Drayton, **founder** of Ashoka, an organization that identifies and invests in social entrepreneurs

2

What is an entrepreneur? The word entrepreneur comes from a combination of the French word *entreprende*, meaning "to undertake," and the English word *enterprise*. Literally, it means "to undertake enterprise." Undertake means to start something and enterprise is a big project. The word *entrepreneur* was invented to describe someone who starts or undertakes a business or enterprise.

The word *business* comes from the Middle English word *bisynesse*. It was first used in the fourteenth century in Europe.

FUN FACT

Most entrepreneurs want to make money, but that's not always the main reason people start their own businesses. Entrepreneurs are **passionate** about their ideas. They believe in them so strongly they are willing to take risks to turn those ideas into reality. Most new businesses do not succeed at first, and entrepreneurs are willing to accept the possibility of failure. In fact, many successful entrepreneurs have created businesses that failed before they finally start one that succeeds.

X-RAY GLASSES HERE

Words 2 Know!

passionate: having strong feelings about something.

persistent: refusing to give up or quit.

An entrepreneur is a person who sees a way to change the world and focuses on accomplishing that change. He or she is **persistent**, willing to take big risks, passionate about his or her project, and focused on achieving goals.

community: a group of people who live in the same area.

BCE: put after a date, BCE stands for Before Common Era and counts down to zero. CE stands for Common Era and counts up from zero. The year this book is published is 2014 CE.

monetary system: the system used by a country to provide money and to control the exchange of money.

goods: things for sale or to use.

Words **2** Know!

Entrepreneurs have been around ever since people first began forming **communities**. Croesus, the king of Lydia in Greece from 560 to 547 **BCE**, was an entrepreneur. He issued the first true gold coins and started the first **monetary system**.

Marco Polo was a famous explorer who traded **goods** around the world. Henry Ford started the first automated car company—your parents might own a car produced by his company. Sir Richard Branson created Virgin Atlantic Airlines. Phil Knight started Nike by making sneakers with a waffle iron and selling them out of the trunk of his car, and Mark Zuckerberg started Facebook from his college dorm room.

These are some of the more famous entrepreneurs. But there are millions of entrepreneurs, all over the world, who have created successful businesses out of their ideas.

Was Columbus an Entrepreneur?

We all know Christopher Columbus sailed the ocean blue to discover the New World (even though he was trying to get to India). But do you think he was an entrepreneur? Let's look at the evidence. He worked for seven years to convince someone rich and powerful to pay for his journey—that takes a lot of passion. He sailed out into the great unknown—that's a huge risk! He refused to turn around even when his crew was on the verge of **mutiny**—that shows great persistence. It sounds as though Columbus certainly possessed some of the key **characteristics** of an entrepreneur!

mutiny: a revolt or rebellion against authority.

characteristic: a feature of a person, place, or thing.

communicate: to share information in some way.

investor: a person who agrees to give time or money to an enterprise.

mentor: a person who advises and guides a younger person.

customer: someone who buys goods or services from a business.

product: an item, such as a book or clothing, that is made and sold to people.

service: work done by one person for another person.

partner: a person who shares the work and reward of a business.

Words 2 Know!

Do you want to become an entrepreneur? There are a lot of different things to think about. You need to start with an idea. How are you going to **communicate** your idea to other people, including **investors**, **mentors**, and **customers**? You need to figure out how to pay for everything you need to operate your business before you start selling your **product** or **service**. Are you going to have a **partner** or employees?

In this book, you'll find out about all the details you need to consider when making decisions about your new business. Are you ready to become an entrepreneur? Let's go!

Chapter 1

Entrepreneurs and Business

Business touches every part of your life, from school and clothing to sports and entertainment. We have the things we need and want, such as televisions, organic strawberries, and bubble gum-flavored toothpaste, because an entrepreneur formed a business that makes and sells those things.

Businesses begin with an idea. But they succeed because of the efforts of an entrepreneur who keeps the business focused and growing. Do you have an idea for a business? Are you an entrepreneur?

Have you ever heard the expression, "Think outside the box?" This means finding **creative solutions** to problems. For example, imagine that you sleep through your alarm clock every morning. You can't help it! It rings, you turn it off, and go right back to sleep. By the time your parents finally wake you up an hour later, you're nearly late for school and don't have time for breakfast.

creative: using imagination to come up with new ideas or things.

solution: an answer to a problem.

opportunity: a chance to do something.

Words 2 Know!

How would you solve the problem? Buy a louder alarm clock? Buy a second alarm clock? Ask your parents to wake you up earlier and hope they remember? Put your alarm clock in a metal trash can where its sound is magnified and you can't reach it from your bed? Some of these solutions are more creative than others. People who come up with creative solutions are the people who think outside the box.

Thinking outside the box is one thing that entrepreneurs do really well.

Entrepreneurs are faced with lots of problems every day, but they don't see problems as bad things. Instead, they see problems as **opportunities** to make their products or services even better. Entrepreneurs rarely say, "I just can't do this," or "This is too hard, I quit." They say, "What happens if we try it this way?" and "Let's change the way we do this."

Business Bio: George Washington

You know George Washington as the first president of the United States, but did you know he was also a very successful entrepreneur? At a time when almost all plantations in the South were growing tobacco, Washington decided to grow wheat and build a mill at his home, Mount Vernon. This worked out well for him. Every year he was able to grind 278,000 pounds (126,099 kilograms) of flour in his mill and ship it all over the colonies and even as far as England and Portugal. After his presidency, he built a distillery, a factory that produced alcohol from crops he grew on his plantation. Even if Washington had never been president, we would still remember his name today because of his business success.

inventor: a person who makes something new.

engineer: someone who uses science, math, and creativity to design and build things.

Words 2 Know!

Entrepreneur or Inventor?

Many of the products we use today exist because an entrepreneur brought them to the public. Do you have an iPod? Steve Jobs is the entrepreneur you can thank for that. He didn't actually invent the iPod or Apple computers. His friend Steve Wozniak was the **inventor** who figured out how to make personal computers for classrooms and homes. Later, it was the **engineers** working for Steve Jobs who created the iPod.

vision: an idea of what we want in the future.

Words 2 Know!

Jobs was able to predict that people would really want to buy Apple computers and iPods. He formed a link between the inventor, the investors, and buyers of his product. His **vision** became the business we know today as Apple.

Entrepreneurs are sometimes inventors, but not always. And inventors are sometimes entrepreneurs, but not always! Inventors are able to create new products, but they aren't always good at recognizing when or how their inventions might appeal to other people. When Steve Wozniak was working to invent the personal computer, he was doing it because it was fun. Then Steve Jobs came along. He believed the computer was something many other people would want to buy.

STEVE AND WOZ'S EXCELLENT ADVENTURES

Entrepreneurs are very good at realizing when something new is going to be attractive to lots of people. They are also good at talking to people about a new invention and at organizing all of the different parts of a business. An entrepreneur can do all of these things while staying focused on his or her vision.

9

wireless: a device that can work without wires.

earbud: a small headphone that fits in the ear.

press release: an official announcement sent to newspapers or magazines.

PowerPoint: a computer program used for making slide-show presentations.

presentation: an activity in which someone shows, describes, or explains something to a group of people.

founding: the group of people that starts a business.

financial: having to do with money.

Words 2 Know!

Many successful businesses are started by a small group of people. Imagine an inventor creates a new kind of **wireless earbud**. An entrepreneur thinks, "Wow, thousands of people will want to buy this!" He or she talks to investors, who contribute money to start the business in hopes of earning back even more money when the earbuds start to sell.

Maybe another person gets involved who's really good at communicating. This person writes commercials and **press releases** and creates **PowerPoint presentations**. Another member of the **founding** group might be talented at math. This person can handle the numbers, the **financial** side of the business. Someone good at design, maybe the inventor, can be the engineer who keeps improving the product.

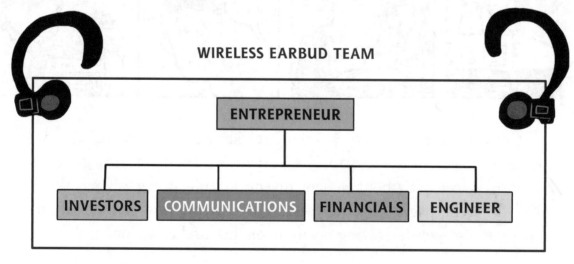

WIRELESS EARBUD TEAM

ENTREPRENEUR

INVESTORS — COMMUNICATIONS — FINANCIALS — ENGINEER

Entrepreneurs and Business

An entrepreneur brings together a team of people with different skills to do all of the jobs necessary to make a business work.

There are lots of different parts to a successful business. Sometimes the entrepreneur can be all the parts, and sometimes he or she needs help. One thing all entrepreneurs have is something called vision. That's vision beyond being able to see what's in front of you. Entrepreneurs are always trying to see farther, to see what people will be interested in tomorrow, to see what problems need to be solved next month or what challenges will arise next year. Sometimes it seems as though they can see into the future.

One Marshmallow or Two?

In the late 1960s and early 1970s, psychologists at Stanford University performed an experiment with a group of preschoolers. They were trying to learn whether children who could wait for a larger reward were more successful as adults. Waiting for the larger reward is called delaying gratification. The researchers put one marshmallow on the table in front of each child and said he or she could eat it right now, but if they waited for 15 minutes without eating it, they'd get another marshmallow as a reward. Some children gobbled up their marshmallows right away, but others worked hard at waiting. A few of them even hid their eyes or turned to face the corner so they couldn't see the yummy food! Follow-up studies have shown that those children who could wait got better grades in school.

Entrepreneurs must often delay gratification when starting a business. For example, they may choose not to take any money from the business earnings at first and instead put that money back into their companies to make them more successful. They are willing to bet on the possibility of a larger reward later on.

Words 2 Know!

option: a choice.

instant camera: a camera that prints the photograph immediately after it's taken.

motivating: giving someone a reason to do something.

increment: a small part of something bigger.

Risky Business

Imagine your mom says, "You have a choice. I'll pay you $5 to wash the car and it can take as long as you want. Or, I'll pay you $10 to wash the car and it has to be done in half an hour. If you take longer than half an hour, I don't pay you anything." Which **option** would you choose?

Entrepreneurs would probably choose the second option—they'd try to complete the job within half an hour and get paid $10 instead of $5. It's a risk. If they can't do the job in half an hour, they get nothing for their work. But if they accomplish their goal, they get twice the money.

Entrepreneurs are not afraid of risk. For them, risk is **motivating** because it makes them work harder to succeed. Some entrepreneurs risk thousands of dollars and maybe even their homes to follow ideas they believe in.

Edwin Herbert Land was the cofounder of the Polaroid Corporation, which produced **instant cameras.** He once wore the same clothes for 18 days while working on an especially challenging project!

FUN FACT

Savvy Source

"One man gets only a week's value out of a year while another man gets a full year's value out of a week."

—Charles Richards, psychotherapist and corporate leadership trainer

Time Keeps Ticking

If you're going to wash your mom's car in only half an hour, you have to organize your time. You can't take 10 whole minutes to wash one hubcap. Consider breaking down the entire job into smaller time **increments**.

Five minutes to get the car wet, 10 minutes to soap it all over, another 10 minutes to rinse, and the last five minutes to catch any spots you missed. Ten dollars coming up!

An entrepreneur handles his or her time in the same way. They understand that each day contains only 24 hours, and every one of those hours has to count when you're starting a business—even if eight of those hours go to sleeping.

Time management is an important part of starting a business. This is especially true if you have other **obligations**, such as another job or school.

Words 2 Know!

obligation: something that must be done.

fee: an amount of money paid for a service.

tax: money charged by a government.

What Is Business?

There are lots of different kinds of businesses, but they all have some of the same qualities. Businesses provide goods or services in exchange for payment. The grocery store sells food for money. The garbage company takes your garbage away for a **fee**. Your school provides an education and is supported by town and state **taxes**. Every good or service provided involves some kind of exchange.

A business can be very small—just one person—or it can consist of thousands of people working all over the world. Businesses can make small amounts of money or billions and billions of dollars.

Grit

You may have heard your parents or teachers talking about something called grit. They're not referring to the crunch between your teeth after a day at the beach! They're talking about the ability to keep trying even after failure. Other words for grit include persistence and determination.

For some people, failure is the last step in starting a business, doing well in school, or performing a cartwheel. They try, they fail, and then they stop trying. But failure doesn't have to be the last step. James Dyson, who invented the Dyson vacuum cleaner, tried 5,127 failed designs during 15 years. Finally he designed the vacuum that would cause a revolution in the vacuum cleaner industry and make him very rich. If he had given up after his first failure, or even his 4,000th failure, he never would have been successful.

Failing can feel awful. Nobody likes it. You might feel embarrassed, confused, or angry. You might have lost your confidence. Everyone who fails at something—which is everyone—feels like this at some point. The best way to heal from those feelings is by trying again.

Even if grit doesn't come naturally to you, you can learn to be persistent in the face of failure. You know you have grit when you keep reaching for success, even when the world seems to say no.

SAVVY SOURCE

"I can accept failure, everyone fails at something. But I can't accept not trying."

—Michael Jordan, basketball player

Early Business

Businesses have been around for thousands of years, even though they weren't called businesses. Long ago, people discovered they could get what they needed more **efficiently** by trading what they had for what they wanted.

Words 2 Know!

efficient: wasting as little time or effort as possible when completing a task.

Imagine a group of early humans. One of them may have been a very talented hunter. Another might have been really good at **foraging** for the kinds of roots and berries that weren't poisonous. The hunter could trade meat for the berries, and both early humans would be happier and healthier. This kind of business is called **bartering**.

forage: to collect food in the wild.

barter: to trade one item for another item.

Oceania: a large group of islands in the South Pacific.

durable: lasting a long time.

miller: someone who grinds wheat into flour.

Words 2 Know!

In a barter system, people exchange items they have for items they need.

For many centuries, cowry shells were used as money in large parts of Asia, Africa, **Oceania**, and smaller parts of Europe. These shells were easy to carry, difficult to fake, and they were **durable**— the perfect money!

FUN FACT

Early American settlers exchanged weapons and spices for food and fur from Native Americans. A European shoemaker traded a new pair of shoes for a bag of flour from the local **miller**. Bartering was how people got what they needed without having to produce everything themselves.

profit: the money made by a business after all **expenses** have been paid.

expense: the amount of money needed to pay for or buy something.

currency: money or other valuable item used for exchange.

credit: paying for something later or over time.

Words 2 Know!

Some people realized that they could even end up with a product or service of higher value than what they started with. They could trade a pair of shoes for a goat, and than trade the goat for a horse, and then trade the horse for a potato field. Early entrepreneurs made connections and realized they could help their communities be healthier and more efficient while making **profits** for themselves.

Eventually, communities started using **currency** to pay for items they needed. Currency can be many different things—cattle, precious metals such as gold and silver, or shells. Today, we use paper money and **credit**. Currency is whatever a community or a government decides is worth something. Businesses sell products and services for this currency.

Local to Global

Local businesses were the first businesses to develop. Think of an early town. One person operated a general store, another person was the blacksmith who made horseshoes and metal tools, and another person was the tailor who made clothing. These business people all performed a service or provided a product that other people in the town needed and were willing to pay for.

16

As towns grew and **transportation** became easier, some businesses grew to serve larger areas. Because communication wasn't always reliable before the Internet and cell phones, business people who bought and sold items in different towns might charge different prices every time. Or they might sell products that weren't very good quality. Customers had to stay aware to make sure they were getting a good deal.

Eventually, business grew to encompass different regions and countries. Today, the world is connected by constant, speedy communication. So it's not unusual for even small businesses to work with people on the other side of the globe.

transportation: a way of moving people and things.

consumer: a buyer of goods or services.

trade route: a route used to carry goods from one place to be sold in another.

global: all over the world.

Words 2 Know!

The Spice of Life

Most households have all the spices they need in the kitchen cabinet, but spices such as cinnamon, cardamom, and ginger used to be very rare and valuable. Spices only grew in remote areas of Asia and Africa and had to be transported on long journeys by camel and ship to **consumers** in Europe and America. The people who controlled the **trade routes** controlled the movement of the spices. They could charge very high prices since there was no other way for people to get spices. This system led to **global** exploration and the discovery of new lands as countries tried to find different ways of reaching the spices everyone wanted.

17

In the Business of Changing Lives

Business is part of our lives and has been for many hundreds of years. **What would the world look like without business?**

The fur trade is one example of how a business altered the course of an entire population. European traders came to North America and offered goods such as weapons, blankets, and liquor to the Native Americans in exchange for animal furs. The traders often worked for large companies such as the American Fur Company, which delivered the furs to consumers in Europe.

How do you think life changed for the Native Americans, who began hunting with rifles instead of bows and arrows? How were their lives different because they traded for wool blankets rather than make them out of animal skins? How did their lives change after alcohol became part of their diet?

The word *buck*, which is slang for a dollar, came from colonial times, when deer fur, called *buckskin*, was traded for goods.

FUN FACT

Later in history, Henry Ford changed the world by making cars more affordable. Ford used an **assembly line** to make his cars so they could be built more quickly and therefore cost less.

In 1910, there were only about 500,000 cars and trucks in the United States. Ford's Model T rolled off the assembly line in 1913 and was inexpensive enough that most people could afford it. By 1920, there were 7.5 million cars and trucks in the United States. How did Ford's business change the way people lived in the United States?

Savvy Source

"Nothing is particularly hard if you divide it into small jobs."

—Henry Ford, American automobile maker

18

Words 2 Know!

assembly line: an arrangement of workers and tasks in a line that make assembling products faster.

The Dutch East India Company

The Dutch East India Company is considered the first **international** business. It was created in 1602 by a group of **merchants** in the Netherlands who wanted to be part of the spice trade. These merchants raised money by selling **shares** of the company, which meant that many people paid money to buy a very small piece of the company. When the company made a profit, the owners of the shares, or **shareholders**, each received part of that profit.

The East India Company lasted nearly 200 years and changed the course of history for many countries. Not only did the company **monopolize** the spice trade, it also **colonized** areas of Asia and Africa and claimed the people who already lived in those places as slaves.

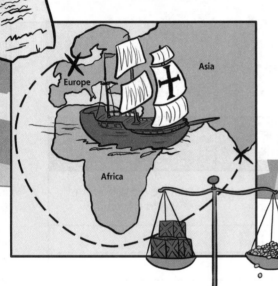

Today, there are lots of rules and **regulations** about how businesses can operate. Local and national governments have laws that are supposed to keep businesses from doing harm. Part of the job of an entrepreneur is to make sure a new business follows the rules while still trying to create something new and useful.

international: happening in more than one country.

merchant: someone who sells something.

share: a small part of a business that can be sold for money.

shareholder: someone who owns shares of a business.

monopolize: to take over and completely control something.

colonize: to take control of an area and the people who live there.

regulation: an official rule or law.

Words 2 Know!

Chart of Businesses

Supplies: *paper, pencil, ruler*

Business is part of our everyday life. In this activity you'll organize businesses into a chart so it's easier to see how businesses affect your life.

1 Make a chart like the one shown below and fill in column one with several different items you find around a specific room in your house.

2 Use row one as an example to fill in the rest of the chart.

Item	Product or Service	Business Name	Customer	What need does it fill?
book	product	Nomad Press	children, parents, and teachers	educate kids about the world we live in!

THINK MORE:

Now go back and consider each item. How would your life or the world be different if the item didn't exist? Can you think of what people used instead of this item before it was invented? Can you do some research and find out who invented the item and when it was invented? Is there an interesting story behind it?

Time Management Calendar

Supplies: *blank piece of paper, pencil, ruler, lined piece of paper, 3 different colored pencils*

Starting a new business takes time. To be successful, you must know how much free time you have and when that free time occurs during the course of a week. Being organized about your time will allow you to ask your parents in advance to drive you places you need to go. If you want people to help you, you can't ask them last minute!

1 Place the blank piece of paper horizontally in front of you so that the long side is at the top. At the top, write a title for your calendar. Maybe you'll include the name of your business. Maybe you'll simply call your calendar what it is, a time management calendar. It's your choice.

2 Use your pencil and ruler to make a thin column, about a half inch wide (1½ centimeters), down the left side of the paper. Then make seven equal columns on the rest of the paper. Each column is for one day of the week. The thin column on the left is for the time of day.

3 At the top of the thin column, write Time. At the top of each of the seven columns, write the name of one day of the week. You can start with Sunday or Monday at the left and continue until Saturday or Sunday is at the right.

Time	Sunday	Monday	Tuesday	Wednesday	Thursday	Friday	Saturday

CONTINUED ON NEXT PAGE . . .

4 Near the top of your Time column, write the time you wake up every day. At the bottom, write the time you go to bed every night. In between, divide up the time in hours and make a mark for each hour.

5 Use the lined piece of paper to list all of the things that you must do every week. Include the days that the activities take place and the beginning and ending times of each of those activities. For example, if you get on the bus to go to school at 8:00 and get off the bus at the end of the day at 3:00, your entry might be, "School 8:00–3:00." Your list should include anything that you are committed to doing: sports, music lessons, meals with your family, homework, and chores. If you play lacrosse on Mondays, Wednesdays, and Fridays from 4:00 to 5:30, write, "Lacrosse, M,W,F 4:00–5:30." If your family eats dinner together every night at 6:00, write, "Dinner 6:00–6:30."

6 Using this list, fill in your blank calendar in blocks. Start with Monday. Choose a colored pencil for School time and a different color for the other Must Do activities. In the Monday column, make a colored block that represents your school day. Write "School" inside it and mark the top and bottom with the times school begins and ends. Now take your Must Do colored pencil and make blocks to represent the activities you must do on Monday after school. Since lacrosse doesn't start until 4:00, your calendar will have a blank space between 3:00, when you get home, and 4:00, when lacrosse starts. Make sure to add all of the things from your list to your calendar.

MUST DO

SCHOOL   8:00 – 3:00
                      (M–F)

LACROSSE 4–5:30
                    M,W,F

DINNER   6:00–6:30

HOMEWORK   3–5:00 Tu,Th
                        7–9 M,W,F

CHORES   7–8 Tu, Th

TIME	Sunday	Monday	Tuesday	Wednesday	Thursday	Friday	Saturday
7:00 a.m.							
8:00 a.m.							
9:00 a.m.							
10:00 a.m.							
11:00 a.m.							
Noon							
1:00 p.m.							
2:00 p.m.							
3:00 p.m.							
4:00 p.m.							
5:00 p.m.							
6:00 p.m.							
7:00 p.m.							
8:00 p.m.							
9:00 p.m.							

7 You now have a calendar that shows what you must do every week. Take your third colored pencil. This will be your Free Time color. Use it to box all of the times that are not already filled.

8 Step back and look at your calendar. It should now be very clear to you when you have free time during the week. As you begin to plan your business, these are the times that you will be able to use to get your work done. How many hours of free time a week do you have?

USE IT: Post your calendar on your bedroom wall. Or put it at the front of a folder or binder where you plan to keep all of your entrepreneurship activities. You may need to create a new time management calendar every few months. Next time, try creating an electronic calendar using software such as Google Calendar.

Chapter 2

Making a Plan

What's the first thing you do when your family decides to take a road trip? Pack your suitcase? Put extra food in the cat's bowl? Call the post office to hold your mail? Hold on! Before you start to pack, you need to know where you're going, right? A trip to the beach requires very different clothing than a skiing trip in the mountains. You'll need to know how long you're going to be away from home before you ask the post office to hold your mail.

The first step to taking a vacation is deciding where you are going. The next step is looking at a map to find out how to get there. These same rules apply to starting a business. Before you can figure out who might be interested in buying your product or service and how to **advertise** to your customers, you need to know what your business is going to be.

advertise: to attract attention to a product, service, or business.

Words 2 Know!

24

If you love to bake, maybe you'll start a baking business. If you're passionate about soccer, maybe you'll invent a glow-in-the-dark soccer ball so kids can play soccer after dark. Are you great with animals? How about a pet-sitting business?

> The first step in starting a business is to form an idea.

Great Ideas

Starting and running a business takes time. Do you want to spend all those hours thinking about something you're not very interested in? If you are not a fan of spinach, do you want to start a business selling spinach? Being an entrepreneur is hard work, and the best way to succeed at hard work is by being passionate about the work you're doing.

What do you love? Tony Hawk became a professional skateboarder at the age of 14, and turned his love of skateboarding into several successful businesses. Besides starting a skateboard **equipment** company, he created video games. His **charitable foundation** builds skate parks in **low-income** areas all over the United States. Tony Hawk loves his job because he loves skateboarding.

Words 2 Know!

equipment: the things you need for a certain activity.

charitable foundation: an organization that raises and donates money to a specific cause.

low-income: describes a group of people who don't earn enough money to meet basic needs such as food and housing.

25

What makes you excited? It could be sports, art, animals, traveling, or something completely different!

There's another kind of business that you might find exciting. Instead of making an object that people want to own, maybe you are interested in offering a service people will want to pay for.

What happens to all the trash in your house? Maybe it gets picked up by the trash company. The trash company stays in business because people want to pay to have their trash removed from their houses instead of bringing it to the landfill themselves. Who do you call when you need to install a new sink? A plumber goes to work every day helping people with all the pipes and fixtures that carry water in their houses.

Business Bio: William Wrigley Jr.

Have you ever chewed a piece of Wrigley's chewing gum? If so, you've tasted the work of a talented entrepreneur. William Wrigley Jr. started out in his father's business selling soap. He figured that people would be more likely to buy his soap if they got something free with it, so he gave away cans of baking soda with every sale. When he discovered customers were more interested in buying baking soda than soap, he switched to selling just the baking soda. To make baking soda more attractive, he gave away chewing gum. Just like before, customers wanted to buy the chewing gum more than the baking soda! So Mr. Wrigley decided to go into the chewing gum business. Juicy Fruit® and Wrigley's Spearmint® both came out in 1893—we still chew these kinds of gum today!

Can you think of a service you could make a business out of?

Brainstorming

When you sit around chatting with your family or a group of friends, do you find that together you can think more creatively than on your own? You may have been **brainstorming**.

Brainstorming is when a group of people thinks together about one subject. Companies encourage brainstorming among employees. Teachers often have their students spend time brainstorming. Maybe your family brainstorms about where to go for your vacation. Brainstorming is a good way to **generate** ideas. Many minds can be more **productive** than just one!

"My definition of success is doing what you love. I feel many people do things because they feel they have to, and are **hesitant** to risk following their passion."

—Tony Hawk, American entrepreneur

Savvy Source

Words 2 Know!

hesitant: slow to act or speak.

brainstorm: to think creatively and without judgment, often in a group of people.

generate: to create something.

productive: working hard and getting good results.

Working on a team might be a new thing for you. It can be embarrassing to say your ideas out loud in a group of people. Sometimes it's hard to be patient and listen to other people's ideas when you have so many of your own to share.

27

Brainstorming Guidelines

There are some **guidelines** to follow that will help make brainstorming enjoyable and productive for everyone.

- **Make only positive comments.** The goal of brainstorming is to come up with lots of ideas. If someone in the group says things like "That's not a good idea," or "That'll never work," it can make people afraid to speak up.

- **Everyone must participate.** Group members can take turns, write their ideas down to be read by another member, or use a talking stick. A talking stick is an item that gets passed around the group and only the person holding the stick can talk. Make sure everyone gets to hold the stick at some point!

- **Encourage wild ideas.** Crazy ideas are a good exercise for creativity! Even if those ideas never leave the room, they may spark other ideas that will.

- **Write down every idea.** Brainstorming is your chance to get lots of ideas down on paper. Later on you can decide which ideas are the best. For now, write them all down.

- **Go for quantity.** The more ideas you have, the better your chances of finding one that works.

- **Be collaborative, not competitive.** There are no best ideas in a brainstorming session. In addition to thinking up new ideas, try thinking of ways to make a friend's idea even better.

- **Stay focused on the question you are trying to answer.** It's always tempting to talk about things other than the question you are trying to answer when brainstorming. If your friends start chatting off topic, remind them gently why you're all there.

- **Use a white board or poster board to write ideas.** This way everyone can see them. This can generate even more ideas.

Thinking Alone

Everyone can benefit from doing some thinking on his or her own, too. But try sitting at your desk and telling yourself to think up a great idea. Does it work? It might, but usually that's a sure way not to come up with a good idea!

Instead of sitting at a desk, stand on your head. Or stand on one foot. Or jog in place for a few minutes. You can even sit on the floor with your eyes closed and try not to think of anything at all! That might be when the perfect idea hits.

Brains like to have fun, and sometimes those moments of fun are when the best thinking happens.

Some entrepreneurs use **meditation** to help them think of new ideas. Going to a place filled with creativity, such as a museum, play, or concert, can give you new ideas. Entrepreneurs are good at making connections between things that, at first glance, seem to have no relationship to each other at all, like a painting in a museum and a new business idea.

Research has shown that napping and daydreaming are good for creating new ideas. That doesn't mean you can simply snooze your way to **inspiration**! Naps and daydreaming are only really useful after you've spent a lot of time doing the hard work of thinking.

meditation: spending time in quiet thought.

inspiration: having great ideas.

Words 2 Know!

29

You Have an Idea... Now What?

Once you start thinking of business ideas, it might be hard to stop! But you might want to work on just one business idea at a time. How do you pick which idea to turn into a company?

One way is to ask, "How am I the best person to make this business idea work?" Maybe you are a soccer player with a busy daytime schedule and need to be able to practice after dark. Maybe you attached your alarm clock to a metal trash can months ago and know firsthand how well that works to wake you up. Or maybe you notice many families forget to take the garbage to the curb early enough on trash day. Would it be easier for them to pay someone to move it for them? Choose an idea that you have experience with.

How excited are you about your idea? Businesses take months, even years to **establish**. Entrepreneurs spend many hours each day thinking about how to make their ideas work. If you're going to get bored of your idea, you might want to choose a different one. An important characteristic entrepreneurs share is the ability to stick with something.

Words 2 Know!

establish: to set up on a permanent basis.

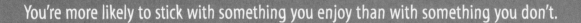
You're more likely to stick with something you enjoy than with something you don't.

Find a Mentor

Starting a business is risky, but you may be able to get help. Mentors are people who have started businesses before and can answer questions about the whole process. You may find that your parents make good mentors, or a teacher, or a neighbor.

Once you have your idea for your business, you get to choose a business name. Think of words that are easy to spell, easy to pronounce, and easy to remember. Use your brainstorming skills to think up a name for your business, and then test that name out on friends and family. Do people like the name? What does it make them think of? Do they remember it?

"I have not failed. I've just found 10,000 ways that won't work."

—Thomas Edison

SAVVY SOURCE

A Plan for Business

Once your family knows where you're going on vacation, what's the next thing you need for your trip? A map! The same goes for starting a business. Once you have your great idea, you need a map, or what's called a **business plan**.

A business plan includes everything you need to do for your business so you don't forget any steps. It's an important **document** that other people will want to look at when they are considering helping you out with your business.

Words 2 Know!

business plan: a written plan that describes how a new business will reach its goals.

document: a written record of something.

31

A business plan keeps you focused and organized. It will help you think and act creatively without losing track of the steps you need to take. It will also help you to decide whether the business you want to start is a good idea. There are a few important parts to a business plan.

Company Overview: Let's say that you decided on the trash can alarm clock as your new business. Congratulations! A company overview is a short, written description about your trash can alarm clock business and why it's going to be successful.

Executive Summary: Who are you and why are you qualified to start this business? Tell people about your experience and background and explain why you decided to start this particular business. If you have partners, include their names and the talents they bring to your business.

Market Research: Who is going to buy your trash can alarm clocks? Teenagers? Parents of teenagers? Families in New England or the Southern states? Are there a lot of these types of consumers in your area? Your **market** is the people you hope to sell your product to. It's important to know your market.

> I was late to school 27 times last year. I just couldn't get out of bed!

market research: the collection of information about people who may become customers.

market: an opportunity for selling, either in an area or to a particular group of people.

attain: to achieve something.

Words 2 Know!

SAVVY SOURCE

"Most great people have **attained** their greatest success just one step beyond their greatest failure."

—Napoleon Hill, American author

32

Industry Analysis: Are there other businesses that sell alarm clocks that might compete with yours? How much do they cost? Is there enough **demand** that more than one business can survive? An **industry analysis** looks at other companies making similar products.

Marketing and Sales Plan: The only way to sell anything is by telling people about it. Once you've figured out a catchy name for your business, you can think of ways to advertise your product to people. All of your ideas will go into your **marketing** and sales plan.

RISE AND CHIME
!!.WAKE UP!!
USE THE BEST ALARM CLOCK TO GET YOU UP IN THE MORNING. DESIGNED TO BE THE BEST AND THE LOUDEST

demand: the amount that people want to buy.

industry analysis: the collection of information about other businesses in a market.

marketing: communicating in different ways to make a business known.

financial projections: the prediction of a company's future expenses and profit.

fund: to pay for.

Words 2 Know!

Financial Projections: It takes money to make trash can alarm clocks. How much money will each one cost you to make? How much will you need to charge your customers in order to make a profit? Keeping track of money is an important part of being an entrepreneur.

Funding Sources: You may have heard the saying, "It takes money to make money." Figuring out how to **fund** your new business is very important. You need to buy materials to build your first trash can alarm clock. Do you have money saved up in the bank to buy those materials? If you need to borrow the money, how will you pay it back?

RISE AND CHIME
FINANCIALS
(WHAT STORE TO USE?)
PARTS
CLOCK $8.00
TRASH CAN $12-15
FASTENERS $1.00
SCREWS $1.50
UNIT COST $22.50
?
LABOR
TOTAL PRICE ???

33

concise: giving a lot of information in only a few sentences.

key player: a person who will help you start your business.

Words 2 Know!

Write It Down

Now that you've chosen an idea, what are you going to say when someone asks, "What's your new business?" Let's look first at your company overview and executive summary, and then we'll explore the other parts of your business plan in the following chapters.

In your company overview you'll describe your business. You'll explain why people need trash can alarm clocks, and give good reasons why you are the perfect person to make and sell them. This may be the very first contact people have with your business, so you want the overview to be clear and **concise**. You want them to find your idea so interesting that they read the rest of your business plan.

You will refer back to your company overview many times as you write your business plan. As your business develops and grows, you might rewrite your company overview to better reflect whatever your business turns into. It's the first step of your business plan and a very important part of being an entrepreneur.

You'll need to think about your group of **key players**. Do you have a partner? Entrepreneurs often work in groups of talented people to ensure that every aspect of the business gets taken care of. Your executive summary should include the names of these people.

Do you have a friend who is a great artist? Do you know someone who already has experience with **spreadsheets**? Think about your own strengths and weaknesses, too. Nobody is good at everything. Are you creative with words? Do you enjoy drawing pictures and making advertisements? Are you terrific at math? What about talking to people? Which of these things is harder for you? By combining talents, a group of entrepreneurs may have a greater chance at success.

Another thing to consider when forming a team is **personality**. Do you want to work with someone who has trouble managing his or her time? Just because someone is talented doesn't mean he or she will make a good business partner. Best friends don't always make the best partners. You want to think about how well you'll work together, too.

Words 2 Know!

spreadsheet: an interactive document on the computer that computes and keeps track of numbers.

personality: the characteristics and ways of behaving that make people different from each other.

qualification: a skill or experience that makes someone suited to a particular job.

If you decide to work with partners, add their names and **qualifications** to your executive summary.

Ben Cohen and Jerry Greenfield were best friends who made great business partners. Have you ever had Ben & Jerry's ice cream?

FUN FACT

It's also a good idea to talk with team members about how everyone will get paid. Once you decide how the money will get divided up among the team members, write down the details and have everyone on the team sign the paper. That way, there will be no argument later when your business starts to make money.

Personality Quiz

Supplies: *paper and pencil*

Starting a new business can be a risky. Take this Personality Quiz! Find out what your score means at the end.

1 You and your friends visit a new restaurant for lunch. The special of the day is Alligator Stew. **Do you say:**

a. "I'll have a big bowl of Alligator Stew, please!"

b. "No, thank you. I'll have the hamburger."

c. "I'll take a hot dog and French fries and just a small sample of Alligator Stew to see if I like it."

2 You and your friends are skiing on a mountain you've never been to before. At the top of the mountain, you come across a trail with a sign that says, "Truly Amazing Trail, Experts Only." **Do you:**

a. Shout "Yippee!" and zoom off down the new trail.

b. Continue on to the easier slope you know you can handle.

c. Ski the easier slope and ask about the expert slope at the bottom of the hill. If it sounds like something you can do, you'll try it next time!

3 It's your first day in a new school after moving to a new town. You enter the lunchroom with your tray and look for a place to sit. **Do you:**

a. Join the table in the middle of the room where lots of people are sitting and talking.

b. Choose a table on the very edge of the lunchroom and eat alone.

c. Choose a table where someone you recognize from your class is sitting. It will be easier to make one new friend at a time.

4 A kid at school says he's found a sure way to make lots of money. All you have to do is buy a box of 25 bags of candy from him for $25 and then you can sell the candy for $2 per bag and make $50. **Do you say:**

a. "I'll take two and make $100!"

b. "No, thanks. I'll just put my $25 into a **savings account**."

c. "First, sell me 10 bags of candy so I can see if people will buy them from me. If they do, I'll come back and buy a whole box."

savings account: a bank account for saving money.

Words 2 Know!

Did you answer mostly a?
You are a risk taker!

Did you answer mostly b?
You usually play it safe.

Did you answer mostly c?
You are the kind of person to think through your actions before you take a risk.

TAKE IT FURTHER: When starting a business, why is it good to be a risk taker? Is it ever a bad idea to take risks? What about people who feel more comfortable playing it safe? What skills does this kind of person bring to a new business? Why is it important to think through your actions before committing to something?

American entrepreneur Elon Musk takes huge risks. He cofounded the online business PayPal and has used money from that success to fund his new ventures, including a company that produces electric cars and another company that is working to send manned rockets to Mars!

FUN FACT

37

Who Am I?

Supplies: *a friend or parent to help you, 11-by-17-inch piece of white drawing paper, tape, strong light source (such as a desk lamp or floor lamp), pencil, black thin-tipped pen, colored pencils*

Before deciding on your business idea, it is important to know your own strengths. That way you can describe why you are uniquely qualified to start your business. In this activity, you'll think hard about what makes you, you!

1 Stand about 1 foot (30 centimeters) away from a flat, empty wall. Ask your friend to tape the piece of white paper to the wall so that it covers the area behind your head.

2 Ask your friend to set up the lamp so that it shines brightly onto your head and makes a shadow on the paper. Make sure not to look directly into the light!

STOP SQUIRMING!

3 Turn so that one ear faces the wall. Move closer to or farther from the wall to make the shadow of your profile fill the paper. Ask your friend to use a pencil to trace your shadow onto the paper. Stand very still! Do you have a ponytail? Are you wearing a hat? Make sure your friend traces the entire shape of your profile, all the way to your neck.

4 Now it's time to fill in your outline with a map of your strengths and passions.

Ask yourself these questions:

* What do I know how to do?
* What are my skills?
* What are my hobbies?
* What do I love to do?
* What would other people say I am good at? (Ask three people!)
* Where do I like to spend time?

* What do I dream about when I have good dreams?
* What do I like to make with my hands?
* How do I like to help others?
* What makes me feel happy?
* When I have free time, how do I spend it?

5 Decide on ways to include the answers inside your profile outline. How will you organize the information so it makes sense? You can break your profile into sections, use different colors for different categories, add illustrations, or write in different styles. Use a pencil in case you want to make changes.

6 When you are satisfied with the organization and design of your profile map, use the black pen and colored pencils to copy over your writing and illustrate your design. Use the black pen to copy over the outline, too. Don't forget to include your name somewhere!

TAKE IT FURTHER: Put your profile map on your bedroom wall. It will remind you of what you love, what you are good at, and how you like to spend your time. These things will be important as you think about your business.

39

Brainstorming Session

Supplies: *4–7 friends or family members, brainstorming guidelines (page 28), Post-it notes, poster board or blank wall, markers*

Brainstorming is a popular technique used in classrooms and companies. Maybe you don't know yet what kind of business you want to start. This project encourages you to think of ideas for new businesses, but you could also use brainstorming for anything, such as ideas on where to go for vacation or topics for your science project—or to find the perfect name for your new business.

1 Everyone in the group gets five Post-it notes and a marker to write down five different ideas for new businesses. Ideas can be strange, funny, outrageous, or serious. Some people find that setting a timer can be a fun way to make ideas flow more quickly!

2 Take turns sticking the Post-it notes to the poster board or wall. Each member should read his or her ideas out loud.

3 How can you group the ideas together? Are there any ways of grouping the ideas that are surprising to you? Do you get more ideas from moving the Post-it notes around?

4 Give everyone one of the Post-it notes, making sure they don't get their own. Can each come up with a way to take that idea further? For example, if someone has an idea for a glow-in-the-dark soccer ball, maybe someone else will expand that idea into a soccer ball that glows in the dark and plays music. Use your imagination!

SAVVY SOURCE

"The way to get good ideas is to get lots of ideas, and throw the bad ones away."

—Dr. Linus Pauling, American scientist

5 Have everyone write down their new ideas and stick these on the poster board with the old ones. Do some more sorting. Do you get more ideas from making new groups?

6 Sit back and look at the poster board. Everyone should choose the three ideas they think are the best and copy them onto three new Post-its. Ask everyone to stick these final Post-its on one corner of the poster.

7 Which ideas were selected? Were any of them chosen by more than one person?

TRY THIS: Use brainstorming whenever you want to think creatively about your business. What are you going to call your business? What sort of advertising are you going to use? Questions such as these can be answered through brainstorming.

Meditation has been shown to affect bodies as well as minds. Studies show that people who meditate sleep better, eat healthier, feel less stressed, and get better grades!

FUN FACT

Evaluating Your Business Ideas

Supplies: *paper, pencil, ruler*

You're on your way to becoming an entrepreneur! Now that you have brainstormed ideas, a criteria chart will help you choose the best one. Entrepreneurs ask many questions when evaluating a problem. Often, they come up with a series of criteria to evaluate their ideas. These criteria are standards or statements that the entrepreneur believes must be true in order for the business to be successful. In this activity, you will develop between three and five criteria that you believe are important. After you consider the criteria in relation to each business, you will be able to make a decision about which business makes the most sense for you.

1 Create a grid like the one below. In the boxes across the top of the grid, write the three possible business ideas you came up with in the previous brainstorming activity.

	Car Wash		
requires few materials	5		
not much driving involved	5		
TOTAL	10		

2 Write your criteria in the boxes down the side of your grid. What do you believe are the important factors for a successful business? This will be different for every entrepreneur. Some of the criteria might have to do with the time it takes to make a product, how easy it is to get the materials you need, whether the product you make will be useful, if it is recyclable, or if it helps people in need. For example, you might write, "I need to be able to make 20 of these items between the end of school and dinner," or, "Requires my parents to drive me somewhere only once a week," or, "When someone throws this away, every part will be easily recycled."

3 Rate your business ideas in relation to your criteria. Use a number scale from 0 to 5. If the answer to something is very true, it gets the highest score, a 5. If it is not true at all, it gets a 0. In the example, "Car Wash" gets a score of 5 for the criterion of "requires few materials" because you only need soap, rags, and a bucket to run this business.

competition: an event at which different teams or individuals compete against each other for an award.

Words 2 Know!

4 To score your grid, add up the values in each column and write the sum in the box at the bottom to find the total. The business with the highest score meets your criteria most closely. This is the business for you!

Many universities around the world sponsor business plan competitions. Young entrepreneurs present their business plans, get advice from leaders in the field, and sometimes win funding for their businesses. Massachusetts Institute of Technology has held a competition for the past 24 years where students can win up to $100,000 for their new business.

FUN FACT

Supplies: *paper, pencil, computer*

Now that you've decided on an idea for a new business, take some time to write an outstanding company overview for your business plan.

1 A company overview is a short, written description about your product or service and why your company will succeed. Try to keep your overview brief, just a few sentences long. This may seem easy, but remember, each sentence must to be concise and powerful. It must catch the attention and imagination of the reader.

2 Have one or more friends or family members review your company overview and offer their thoughts. You may want to do some more work on the company overview to get it just right. Revise!

COMPANY OVERVIEW EXAMPLE

Rise and Chime

Rise and Chime trash can alarm clocks are perfect for busy families who need to wake up early for school and work. Louder than traditional alarm clocks, a trash can alarm clock jolts you awake with a loud ring magnified by its placement on a metal can. Rise and Chime is founded by kids who know how tough it can be to get out of bed.

Executive Summary

Supplies: *pencil, paper*

It's time to take what you have learned about yourself and use it to write your executive summary. Why did you decide to start this particular business and what makes you the perfect person to do it successfully? Don't forget to use descriptive vocabulary and active verbs! Just as with your company overview, have other people read it over and make suggestions.

EXECUTIVE SUMMARY EXAMPLE

I was late to school 27 times last year. Why? Because I couldn't claw my way out of bed in the morning! But then I showed initiative and created the very first trash can alarm clock. With my dedication to quality and results, I am the perfect person to stand at the helm of the Rise and Chime Trash Can Alarm Clock Company.

Words 2 Know!

incandescent: containing a wire that glows when heated by an electric current.

Failure?

Thomas Edison was famous for a lot of different inventions, including the **incandescent** light bulb and the phonograph, which was an early music player. He also invented a lot of things that never became useful. You've probably never heard of his Kinetophone, used by one person to watch a motion picture. When your ideas don't work well, do you feel like quitting or working harder? Why?

Chapter 3

Customers and Competition

You may be eager to start building lots of trash can alarm clocks and start selling. But first you need to find answers to a few questions: How much does it cost to make your product? How long does it take to make it? Are there people willing to buy trash can alarm clocks and how much will they pay for one? Are other companies making the exact same thing? How is your product going to be different?

As an entrepreneur, you need to be able to make your product for less than what you charge for it. You need to know who your customers are going to be and who your **competition** is. You need to know your market. Building a **prototype** and completing a few more steps in your business plan will help you to understand your product and your market before diving into production.

Words 2 Know!

competition: a person or company or group that you are trying to succeed against.

prototype: a first or early model of something new.

46

Make Your Prototype

If your business is one that sells a product, you need a good prototype of that product. You might have already made a prototype as part of discovering your talent as an entrepreneur! Many people create a product for their own use before it occurs to them to try to sell it to other people.

If you don't have an example of your product yet, it's time to construct a prototype. If you already have a prototype, it's still a good idea to go through the process again to work out any problems. Make a plan for building your item and write a list of supplies and what each one costs. Build your product, and then fix any problems you discover in the process.

Business Bio: Leanna Archer

When Leanna Archer was eight years old, her friends asked her all the time how they could have hair that looked like hers. Leanna used a hair care product made with a recipe created by her grandmother, who was from Haiti. She gave lots of her product away for free, and then started selling it in baby food jars. Her business was born—Leanna's Natural Hair Products. As she created more hair care products, Leanna sold them in stores and online. By age 18, Leanna was the **chief executive officer (CEO)** of a global business.

Words 2 Know!

chief executive officer (CEO): the highest-ranking person in charge of a company.

reduce: to use less of something.

feedback: helpful information or criticism given to improve something.

survey: a series of questions asked to gather information.

Words 2 Know!

How can you make the building process as efficient as possible? How can you get your materials at the least expensive price? Even established companies spend a lot of time trying to **reduce** the cost of making their products.

The less money you spend on production, the more money you make after selling your product.

You'll want to test your prototype out on friends and family members to make sure it's worth selling. Maybe you've built a super powerful trash can alarm clock, but when your best friend tries it out, it's so loud that it scares the dog. You might want to make a quieter version that's still loud enough to wake up teenagers. **Feedback** from people who try out your product will be extremely valuable.

You can get feedback by asking the people who try your product to fill out a **survey**. Can you think of some questions you can ask that will give you good information to help you improve your product? Keep it short, between seven and ten questions, or your survey takers might get bored and leave the survey unfinished!

You can ask people to rate your product on a scale of one to ten or to give you a list of things they like and another list of things they don't like about your product. Once you have feedback from several people, you may want to change the design of your prototype to solve the problems your friends and family members found.

Words 2 Know!

social media: websites where people can write messages to each other.

Online Surveys

You can also create surveys online. Always check with an adult before you use the Internet. Try www.surveymonkey.com to create a survey to send through email or **social media**. Google also has a program called Forms. It's a good idea to create an email address just for your business instead of using your personal email address to create surveys. You can create free email accounts at Gmail or Yahoo.

An important part of making your prototype is keeping track of both the time and the money you spend on it. You need to know how much it costs to buy all of your materials and how much time you spend designing and building your product. If your brother spends an hour helping you with the hot glue gun in exchange for you walking the dog, which is usually his chore, keep track of that, too.

Spreadsheets are a great way to keep track of all the time and money you spend on your prototype. You can use a spreadsheet on a computer or make your own. If you use the computer, the program will be able to do a lot of the math for you. We'll learn more about spreadsheets in chapter 4.

Service!

Let's say you've noticed that a lot of people in your neighborhood have trouble getting their heavy trash cans to the curb in time for the garbage truck on Thursday morning. *Aha!* Here's a good business idea!

But wait—how long will it take you to bring a single trash can from a house to the curb? How many house-to-curb trips can you do in an hour? How early will you have to get up on Thursday morning to transport all the trash cans in your neighborhood?

If your neighborhood is a large one, it's possible that you'll need to use a bike or get a ride from someone to visit all your customers. In that case, you'll need to think about transportation costs. Maybe you already have a bike and helmet, but if your mom needs to drive you when it rains, you might have to pay her for the gas. What if your bike gets a flat tire that needs repairing?

Costs such as these need to be considered as you decide what to charge your customers.

Cheaper by the Dozen

Have you ever read the book *Cheaper by the Dozen*? The parents, who had 12 children, were real people who were interested in **motion study** and **scientific management**. Frank and Lillian Gilbreth tried to make every action as efficient as possible, whether they were building a brick wall or making dinner for a large family. How can you make your motions more efficient when building your prototype or delivering your service? Try timing yourself while you perform your service. Then try doing it a different way that takes less time. Can you deliver the same quality of service in less time?

PS Watch the films made by the Gilbreths during their experiments in scientific management. How do you think people reacted to their discoveries?

motion study: finding the most efficient way of performing a job.

scientific management: the management of a business to increase efficiency.

nonprofit business: an organization focused on improving a community in some way. It relies on donations to pay its costs.

Words 2 Know!

Who Are You Selling To?

Every business has one thing in common: customers! Without customers, your business doesn't succeed. Customers are a crucial part of every business. Even **nonprofit businesses** that aren't trying to make a profit need customers or someone to provide services for. A nonprofit business that helps people who are homeless considers homeless people to be its customers. Without homeless people, the nonprofit business has no reason to exist.

51

It's a good idea to know as much as you can about the people who might want to buy your product or service. Can you think of ways to find out if people will buy your trash can alarm clock? **How do you know if there's a market for your product?** Most entrepreneurs use market research to learn about their customers before they spend too much time and money trying to make a business work.

Savvy Source

"Spend a lot of time talking to customers face to face. You'd be amazed how many companies don't listen to their customers."

—Ross Perot, American entrepreneur

Introvert or Extrovert?

What do Bill Gates, Emma Watson, and Albert Einstein all have in common? They are all introverts! Introverted people get energy from being alone. Extroverted people get energy from being with other people. Most people are a combination of these two personality types. Introverts are often uncomfortable meeting storeowners, handing out surveys, and talking to future customers. Extroverts often have an easier time with things like that.

Many successful business leaders are introverts who have learned how to be their best even when they are in large groups of people. They know to take breaks to recharge and to feel confident about taking time to think before answering questions. If you are an introvert, what are some strategies you can use when meeting with other people?

Characteristics of an Introvert

- does not like big parties
- gets distracted easily
- people describe you as quiet

Characteristics of an Extrovert

- likes big parties
- gets bored easily
- enjoys meeting lots of new people

52

Town Annual Reports

Have you ever visited your town or city offices? You may have gone there with your parents to register a car or renew your dog's license. Town and city offices are very busy places that collect and keep track of lots of interesting information about where you live. Much of that information can be found in the town annual report.

Small towns may publish one complete report every year that contains all the information you might find interesting for your business. Big cities such as New York City or Los Angeles may have several different annual reports to cover topics such as **demographics**, **financial reports**, and updates on **recreation programs**. If you need help finding information on the demographics of your town, ask the people who work at the town offices or a local librarian. They can show you where to find the information you're looking for.

Words 2 Know!

demographic: a group of people that shares the same qualities, such as age or gender.

financial report: an official record of the financial activities of a business or organization.

recreation program: a program designed to encourage people to have fun and relax.

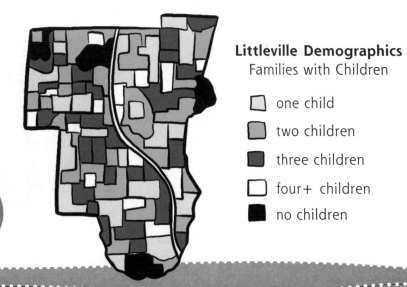

Littleville Demographics
Families with Children

☐ one child
☐ two children
☐ three children
☐ four+ children
■ no children

Be prepared to explain your business idea and why you want the information you are looking for. This is another great opportunity to practice describing your company in a clear and concise manner. Adults will want to help you if you are polite, clear, and eager to learn.

As an entrepreneur, you will be most interested in the report on demographics. Where people live, their ages, whether they live alone or in families—all of these topics will help you know whether or not you'll have customers for your new business. **Why do you need to know the ages of people living in your town?** How will this information help you?

Words 2 Know!

census: an official count of the people living in a country.

The Country at a Glance

You'll want to conduct market research at the local level, but it can be fun to explore the demographics of the entire country. Every 10 years the United States Census Bureau does a **census**. Every family in the country answers question on a census form so that the Census Bureau can count how many people live in the United States. The census records ages and other information, such as how much money people make every year and whether they live in the country or the city.

PS You can access census information online.

All of the people in your town's annual report are potential customers. But only some of them will be interested in a trash can alarm clock. A retired man in his seventies who lives alone and doesn't have to wake up early to go to a job probably won't need a trash can alarm clock. What about a family with three kids ages 8, 10, and 15 who all have to be at school by 7:30 a.m.? Do you think they are good customers for your product? What are some other groups of people who would find a trash can alarm clock useful?

Check Out the Competition

"I have no friends and no enemies—only competitors."

—Aristotle Onassis, Greek entrepreneur

SAVVY SOURCE

Once you know something about your local market, you'll have an idea of how many people might want to buy your trash can alarm clock. Now you can start thinking about your competition. Other companies have been selling alarm clocks for years, right? What makes your trash can alarm clock special enough to convince customers to try something new?

It's time for more research! In the same way that you did market research, now it's time to perform an industry analysis. This is when you collect information about the companies that sell what you want to sell.

Your first step might be to take a walk or a drive through your town. Which stores seem to be the busiest? Which businesses can you see that are thriving? You may notice that your local general store has lots of cars in the parking lot and plenty of people going in and out. Maybe the hardware store has a front counter crowded with people.

One of the most famous competitions in business has been between Coca-Cola and Pepsi, which are actually pretty similar drinks.

FUN FACT

Do any of these busy stores sell alarm clocks? Once you've found two or three stores that sell alarm clocks, look at all the alarm clocks for sale.

website: a group of web pages on the Internet that all relate to one business.

keywords: the subject words in a sentence or phrase.

web page: a digital document found on the World Wide Web.

resourceful: able to deal with new or difficult situations and to find solutions to problems.

Words 2 Know!

Where else might people go to buy alarm clocks? Many people shop online to save time and money. Nearly every business has a **website** and reaches its customers through social media.

Doing a **keyword** search for "shop alarm clocks" will bring you to **web pages** that may show the price of different types of alarm clocks and the names of the companies that make them. One of the most popular shopping sites is Amazon. You'll be able to see which alarm clocks sell the best around the world and how much they cost.

Why is it important to do an industry analysis? By exploring your competition, you may get more ideas on how to make your product or service better. You'll also find out how much money other companies are charging for their work. This might help you decide what you should charge for yours.

Business Bio: Markus Persson

Most people know Markus Persson by the name *Notch*. Have you ever played a video game called *Minecraft*? Notch created *Minecraft*, which puts players in a world made of blocks and requires them to survive by being **resourceful**. Notch made up hundreds of games as a kid and worked on even more games as an employee of a large company. When he quit his job to focus on his own games, he had lots of experience. Still, he was shocked when *Minecraft* became so popular. Last year, Notch earned more than $100 million from *Minecraft*!

Making Information Useful

You've read your town's annual reports, had your friends fill out surveys, asked local shop owners about their products, and looked online at companies that sell similar products. What should you do with all of your notes? **Data** is only useful when it's organized. Charts, graphs, and lists are great ways to organize information so you can understand it.

Words 2 Know!

data: information, facts, and numbers.

When you present your data in an organized way in your business plan, it shows investors that you have done your research.

Pie chart: Pie charts are easy to understand and are most often used when comparing parts of a whole. Start with your information about demographics. How many people live in your town? How many of those are ages 0 to 9? How about 10 to 18? How many of them are older than 18?

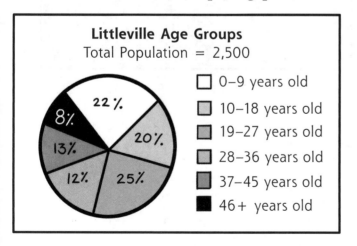

Littleville Age Groups
Total Population = 2,500

- ☐ 0–9 years old
- ☐ 10–18 years old
- ☐ 19–27 years old
- ☐ 28–36 years old
- ☐ 37–45 years old
- ■ 46+ years old

22%, 8%, 13%, 12%, 25%, 20%

You can make a pie chart like this one to show how many people of certain ages live in your town. If there are 2,500 people in your town, a pie chart would be a good tool to use to show the size of each of the different age groups within the population.

57

Bar graph: Bar graphs put data into columns and are best for comparing things between different groups. Maybe you found that alarm clocks ranged in price from $7.55 to $30.50. You can compare the different brands and prices by using a bar graph.

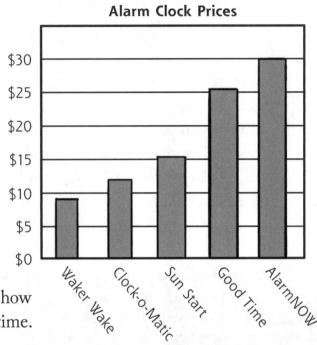

Alarm Clock Prices

Line graph: A line graph uses lines and points to show how information changes through time. Perhaps you found out that alarm clock sales have increased every year during the last 10 years. You can use a line graph to show how the sales have increased each year, which will help you show that the market for clocks is growing.

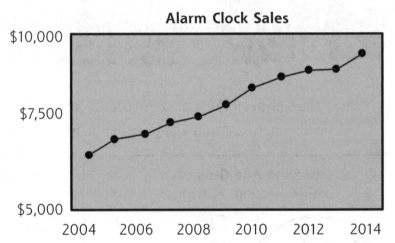

Alarm Clock Sales

Now What?

You've conducted your market research, done your industry analysis, and made your charts and graphs to organize your data. Now what? Review all your data. Based on the information you have collected, do you think your business will be successful?

Let's say you now know that 1,500 out of 4,000 people living in your town are children between the ages of 6 and 18 who need to wake up early to get to school. Only two stores sell alarm clocks, and none of their alarm clocks are loud enough to get kids out of bed. It looks as though you have a great environment for a trash can alarm clock business!

> "Research is formalized curiosity. It is poking and prying with a purpose."
>
> —Zora Neale Hurston, American author

SAVVY SOURCE

14-year-old Seth Priebatsch had a lemonade stand in Boston, Massachusetts, that made $500 a day! He and his friends got a **permit** to sell on Newbury Street, a busy street filled with potential customers. Seth went on to start four different companies before college and is the creator of a very popular video game called SCVNGR.

FUN FACT

What if you discover that only a small part of the population has to get up early? And five stores already sell really loud alarm clocks? Do you think your trash can alarm clock business will be successful?

Now you have a decision to make. You can make a prototype and try to get people interested anyway. Or you can move on to a different idea. Many entrepreneurs get this far with different business ideas before choosing one that works.

Think about what the people of your town need. Maybe your town has a lot of retired people who have time to go to a monthly music festival. Creating that music festival could be your business! Or perhaps the elderly people in your town need help with daily chores. Sounds like an opportunity to sell a service!

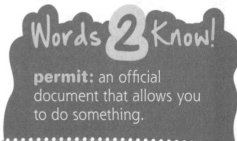

Words 2 Know!

permit: an official document that allows you to do something.

Part of entrepreneurship is gathering information and making decisions based on that information.

Build a Prototype

Supplies: *materials needed to make your product, paper and pencil, computer word document*

There are many reasons to make a prototype. First, you want to know if you can actually make it! If you can't, you'll need to find someone who can or choose a different business idea. Second, you should know how much time it takes to make one of your products. Third, you'll want to know exactly how much it costs to make one of your products. This will help you decide how much you need to charge to make a profit. Finally, making a prototype will allow you to share it with friends and family to make sure it works and to get their feedback on your idea.

1 What will you need to make your product? Make a list of materials. When you shop for the materials, make a note of how much each item costs.

2 Once you have all of your materials, look at your time management calendar. Find a chunk of time that you can use to make your prototype.

3 Get to work! Look at the clock and mark down the time you begin to build your prototype.

4 Build your prototype. When you are finished, look at the clock and mark down the time you finished. Now write down how long it took you to make your product.

5 Share your product with your family and your friends. Ask them for feedback. Then make adjustments to your product and your materials list as necessary.

6 Did it take you a long time to make your prototype the first time? If you think you could do it more quickly a second time, make a second prototype and time yourself.

7 Take a photograph of your product to include in your business plan.

TRY THIS: If your business will provide a service rather than goods, you'll still need to keep track of your expenses, the time it takes to do the job, and the time it takes to travel between jobs. Make sure to record the price of the materials you use and time yourself as you perform the service. If you need to be driven to locations, remember that gas costs money, too!

Numbers 2 Know

If your prototype needs one popsicle stick and popsicle sticks come in bags of 10, divide the cost of a bag of popsicles by 10 to find out the cost of one popsicle stick.

$$\frac{\$3 \text{ (cost of one bag of popsicle sticks)}}{10 \text{ (number of popsicle sticks in each bag)}} = 30¢ \text{ (cost of each popsicle stick)}$$

Take a Survey

Have you ever taken a survey? Surveys are a great way to get honest feedback from your friends and family, but it might be a good idea to take one yourself first so you know what to expect. Take the following survey to discover which Hogwarts House you belong to and then create your own survey!

1 When faced with an enemy on a deserted road at night, **you:**

a. Try to walk past, ready to defend yourself if necessary

b. Stand aside and wait patiently for your enemy to leave

c. Challenge them to a battle of wits

d. Trick your enemy into turning his or her back, then hitting him or her on the head with a rock

2 How often do you rescue a stranger in need?

a. Whenever I can

b. Only if I won't get hurt

c. Once a month, like clockwork

d. Never

3 When given the following choices for dinner, **which would you pick?**

a. Bouillabaisse (a fish stew)

b. Chicken soup with real chicken broth

c. Vegetable soup

d. Steak soup

4 When faced with an impossible challenge, **you are most likely to:**

a. Get your friends to help you solve it

b. Keep working on the problem until you solve it or it disappears

c. Say there is no such thing as impossible

d. Force whoever created the problem to give you the answer

If you chose mostly a: you belong in Gryffindor.

If you chose mostly b: you belong in Hufflepuff.

If you chose mostly c: you belong in Ravenclaw.

If you chose mostly d: Slytherin is the place to be!

If you chose one of each letter: you get to decide.

SAVVY SOURCE

5 Now create a survey for your friends and family to take after they try your prototype. There are some sample questions below to get you started. What else do you want to know? Tally the answers for each question in charts.

My trash can alarm clock woke me up when I wanted it to.	Disagree	Somewhat Agree	Strongly Agree
My trash can alarm clock was easy to set.	Disagree	Somewhat Agree	Strongly Agree
On a scale of one to five, I rate my trash can alarm clock a	1 - 2 - 3 - 4 - 5		

Market Research

You can also use a survey to do market research before you give out your prototype. What questions do you think will give you the most useful information? Here are a few ideas based on the trash can alarm clock business idea.

★ Do you use an alarm clock?

★ How many times a week do you sleep through your alarm?

★ How many times a week are you late for school or work?

★ How many people in your family use their own alarm clocks?

★ Would you spend $10 on an alarm clock that was guaranteed to wake you?

★ Would you spend $20?

★ Does the size of an alarm clock matter to you?

63

Perform an Industry Analysis

Supplies: *pencil, paper, clipboard*

It's important to know who your competition is. Get out to stores near you and investigate products that might compete directly with your product.

1 Make a chart to organize the names and prices of items that might compete with yours. You'll also want to include a place to write down the comments that business owners might have about specific products.

Item	Name	Price	Store	Notes
alarm clock	Wide Awake Alarm Clock	$25	RadioWorld	Storeowner says doesn't sell well— too expensive.

2 On a different piece of paper, write a brief note explaining that you are conducting industry analysis for your new business. You might be able to use the text you have written for your company overview. This will help you organize what you want to say to a storeowner. Make sure to mention your age. Adults are often more willing to help when they know they are helping a kid do something interesting. Be clear about your request and make sure to remember to thank the business owner for his or her help.

3 Write a list of questions for storeowners to answer about the product you are researching. **Some questions about alarm clocks might include:**

* How many different brands of alarm clocks do you sell?
* Which one sells the best?
* Have customers told you what they don't like about alarm clocks or what they would like?

4 Make copies of your questionnaire so you will have enough to leave at every store you visit. Bring a self-addressed, stamped envelope with each questionnaire to make it easy for the owner to mail it back to you.

5 Visit different stores in your town that sell the product you want to make. Look at the products in the store and record the information in your chart. Ask politely for the manager or owner and use your sheet of questions to ask for more information. If the owner is not there, ask if there is a good time for you to come back or ask where you can leave your questionnaire and envelope for that person. If your parents have given you permission to use a business email account, you can give them your business email address so they can contact you.

6 Ask an adult for permission to search the Internet for more products that might compete with yours. Add the information you find to your chart. Remember to add shipping costs to the price of the item and make a note of this in your chart so you can explain it later to your investors.

Organize Your Data

Supplies: *paper, graph paper, colored pencils, Internet*

Many people find it easier to look at a picture of information rather than reading information in numbers and text. Graphs are effective because they communicate information in a visual manner and people can understand them quickly. Now that you have completed your market research and industry analysis, take some time to make graphs that show what you have found. They will be an important part of your business plan.

1 What type of graph should you use? It depends on the kind of data you want to organize.

* ★ **Pie charts** are most often used when comparing parts of a whole.
* ★ **Bar graphs** are best for comparing things between different groups.
* ★ **Line graphs** show change through time.

2 Follow the examples from pages 57 and 58 to create pie charts, bar graphs, and line graphs for your data. Use a separate sheet of plain or graph paper for each kind of information. Different colors can be useful to make you graphs and charts more interesting and easy to read.

TAKE IT FURTHER: Here are some interesting websites with some ideas on charts and graphs. They can help you make your own. Get your parents' permission to use these websites to create graphs. Cover up neighboring QR codes to make sure you're scanning the right one!

Chapter 4

Marketing and Communication

The world relies on communication. Think of all the **interactions** you have every day. You eat breakfast with your parents, you listen to your teacher, you talk and laugh with your friends, and you follow your coach's instructions on the soccer field.

When you meet a stranger, what do you do? Do you look at his or her eyes, give a firm handshake, and say, "Nice to meet you," in a clear voice? Or do you look at the ground and mumble something he or she can't understand with your hands shoved in your pockets? Which do you think is the more effective way of communicating?

interaction: the action or influence of people, groups, or things on one another.

Words 2 Know!

You've learned that it takes a lot of people to make a business successful. A team of friends and family and mentors will help you develop your idea and invest in your business. Customers will buy your product or service. Without all of these people, your business will be a very lonely enterprise and not very profitable.

How do you connect with all these people and tell them about your business? Through communication and marketing. That is how you achieve your goal, which is to makes sales.

It All Rests on You

You may have to convince your friends to join your business team. You might have to hold a meeting with your mother to ask her to give you a **loan**. You'll definitely have to make presentations to potential investors. You are going to find yourself talking to a lot of people while you start your business.

loan: money that is borrowed and paid back with **interest**.

interest: the fee charged for the use of money in a loan.

Words 2 Know!

The best way to make a successful presentation is to be prepared. That doesn't just mean knowing what you are going to say, though that's important, too! **Can you think of other ways you need to be prepared?**

One way to prepare yourself is to think about your audience. Let's say you have a chance to talk to your uncle, who is thinking about investing money in your new business.

Savvy Source

"The most important thing in communication is hearing what isn't said."

—Peter F. Drucker, American management consultant and educator

68

What will you wear to the meeting? Why is that important? You want to be sure that you aren't wearing something that distracts your audience from what you are saying. If your shirt is ripped or if your feet stink, this may have an effect on your uncle's decision to invest his money.

If you're meeting with a bunch of friends, they may not care at all if your hair is messy. But they will still expect you to be able to talk about your business idea in a clear way. You will need to convince them you're serious about working hard.

Investors take a big risk when they give money to a new business. They want to see that the entrepreneurs they're investing in are taking this risk seriously.

Verbal Communication

draft: an early version of a piece of writing, which will be revised.

Words 2 Know!

It can be frustrating when your teacher makes you write 10 **drafts** of an essay, but there's a very good reason for it. Words matter. You're going to use words to convince the person in front of you that your idea is a great one and that you are the perfect person to bring it to reality.

The way you present your idea matters, too. Mumbling won't get this done. Shrugging? Bad idea. Talking to the floor is a definite no-no. How should you present yourself to make the best possible impression?

Your presentation starts before you get to the meeting. Look back at the company overview you wrote in chapter 2. Your company overview contains the ideas you want to tell your audience. But just reading it out loud to people isn't enough. What can you do with your company overview so that it sounds good when you say your ideas out loud?

Presenting Your Overview

Here are some ideas to get you started on presenting your company overview.

Turn it into a personal story. Everyone loves a story! "Last year, I was late to school 27 times. My mom couldn't wake me up. My little brother couldn't wake me up. Even my sister's hairdryer couldn't wake me up. Want to know the only thing that worked? My trash can alarm clock!" Starting your presentation like this immediately gets people interested in what you have to say.

Write key words on index cards to refer to when you're giving a presentation. This will give your brain a reminder of what you want to talk about and give your hands something to do.

Find some humor to share with your audience. Just as everyone loves a story, everyone loves to laugh, too. Find some funny parts about your experience of starting a business and share them. "Why am I the best person to run this business? Because I sleep harder than anyone else in the world!"

Presentation software such as PowerPoint is a way to create a slideshow. Keep the number of slides in your presentation somewhere between 10 and 20, or they will become distracting instead of helpful.

Use your key words as titles for your slides, and include graphs from your market research, industry analysis, and financial projections. You can even add some photographs of yourself and your team hard at work. Try not to write complete sentences in a slide presentation. You want to tell your story and have visual information on your slides that supports it.

"Audiences forget facts, but they remember stories."

—Ian Griffin, American speechwriter and communications expert

Savvy Source

If you don't have PowerPoint software, you can still make a presentation using large pieces of paper or cardboard. Be creative!

Practice! It may feel strange to talk to yourself in your bedroom, but the more you practice talking about your idea and your plans, the easier it will be when the time comes to do it in front of actual people. Also, think of questions your audience may ask and make sure you know the answers!

Recruit family and friends to listen to you practice. This way you'll know how it feels to talk about your business in front of someone. Ask them to write down three things you do well and three things you need to improve. You can also practice in front of a mirror.

Words 2 Know!

recruit: to get someone to join you or help you.

71

Nonverbal Communication

Words matter in a conversation or presentation, but so does what you do with your hands and your body. **Nonverbal communication** is what the rest of your body is doing while your mouth is talking.

You may not even be aware that you're sending information beyond what you're saying. The person you're talking to may not even know that they're reacting to something other than your words. But how you hold yourself, what you do with your hands, and your **facial** expressions all convey meaning.

Try to keep your facial expression open and interested. If you scowl, frown, or wrinkle your nose, you may be unconsciously saying that you're not happy or that you are nervous. If you smile, meet the other person's eyes, and nod when it's appropriate, other people know that you believe in what you're talking about and are excited for the opportunity to share it.

Nonverbal communication makes up more than two-thirds of every interaction! What do we lose when we rely on texting and email to communicate?

FUN FACT

What about the rest of your body? You will look the most comfortable if you simply keep your hands at your sides, or clasp your hands loosely in front of you. While this might feel awkward, it will look very natural to your audience.

We all have **habits** that can be distracting for other people to look at when we're trying to talk to them. Do you bite your nails? Constantly push your hair away from your face? By becoming aware of our distracting habits, we can work to change them.

One way to keep ourselves from these habits is to breathe deeply when we notice ourselves doing them. This changes our focus and might let us skip the behavior we don't want to do.

Words 2 Know!

habit: a regular behavior that is hard to give up.

Dress to Impress

When you are talking to people and asking questions, remember that you are representing your business. This means that whatever people think of you, they are going to think the same about your business. If you are wearing a ripped T-shirt or if you mumble, look down at the ground, scowl, and forget to say please and thank you, do you think people are going to want to help you? Do you think they will become your customers? Write down what you want to say before you visit places such as the town office or local schools and practice with a friend or family member or in front of a mirror. Remember to dress nicely for your visit!

logo: a symbol used to identify a company that appears on its products and in its marketing.

letterhead: a sheet of stationery printed with the name, address, and logo of a company.

packaging: the wrapper or container that holds a product.

slogan: a phrase used by a business or other group to get attention.

Words 2 Know!

Marketing

Marketing is a special kind of communication for attracting customers to a product or service. Anything your business does that makes people notice your product or service and then buy it has to do with marketing. This includes naming your business, designing a **logo** and **letterhead**, creating **packaging** for your product, and advertising.

Advertising is a very visible form of marketing. When businesses advertise using words and pictures in magazines and newspapers, it's called print advertising. There is also television advertising, online advertising, and billboards. Advertisements use pictures, famous people, catchy songs, and **slogans** to get people to notice and buy certain things. Can you think of other methods that advertisements use to attract us to their products or services?

Coupon Craze

Maybe your parents use coupons to get discounts at the grocery store or maybe your teacher hands out coupons for free books. But did you know that the first coupon ever was for a drinkable treat? In 1887, the Coca-Cola Company gave out about 8.5 million coupons for free drinks of Coke! This marketing strategy made Coke the favorite drink of lots of people across the country.

Business Bio: Jacob Schweppes

Jacob Schweppes, a watchmaker from Germany, started selling fizzy mineral water in 1783. Many people bought his drink because they thought it had healing properties. Schweppes claimed that his drink was responsible for "invigorating the system and exalting the spirits." He sold his company in 1798 and the new owners kept his name for their product. Now, more than 200 years later, we still drink Schweppes, even though we no longer believe it will cure us of disease. In the 1950s and 1960s, advertisers used the fun term "Schweppervescence" to market the drinks.

Why is advertising effective?

Some advertisements make us think our lives could be better if we purchased a particular product. Even just the act of seeing an advertisement over and over can make us want to buy that product. Perhaps the **jingle** that's used in the advertisement gets into our heads and that's what we hear when we go to the store. Then we're drawn to the product that's named in the jingle!

Some advertising appeals to a person's sense of humor. Commercials that make us laugh are the ones we often remember! Advertising can also make us feel smart. If a commercial uses statistics and concrete information about a product, buyers might feel as though they're getting the best deal.

"Effective frequency" refers to how many times a person needs to be exposed to an advertising message before he or she responds to it. Some experts say three, some say seven, and others say 20!

FUN FACT

Words 2 Know!

jingle: a short song used in advertising.

Going Digital

One form of digital advertising is online advertising. Always get a parent's permission before you use the Internet. You can develop a web page for your business and post your company name and logo, your product or service, contact information, pictures of your product, quotes from satisfied customers, and even videos in which your product plays the starring role. There are lots of fun ways to get the word out about your business.

On average, children see more than 40,000 television advertisements every year. That's a lot of chances to make a new customer!

FUN FACT

Many communities now have local digital mailing lists, called **listservs**, for town residents. You may be able to post a simple advertisement there. Check the rules on what's called the **netiquette** page before you advertise. Ask your parents to help you find the email list and post your email. If you have a web page, include a link to it.

Words 2 Know!

listserv: an electronic mailing list.

netiquette: rules of appropriate behavior for the Internet.

Internet Safety

Always get permission before using the Internet, and follow these basic safety rules.

- Never list your home address on any of your materials.

- Don't include pictures of yourself on your website, and get permission from other people before including their pictures.

- Create a separate email address for your business.

- Always assume that anything you put on the Internet is permanent and may be seen by anyone, including teachers, friends, family, and future employers.

e-newsletter: an email newsletter.

advergame: an online game that attracts players to certain products without their knowledge.

dialogue: conversation between characters in a book, movie, or video game.

graphics: pictures and animation.

product placement: putting products in movies or television shows as a form of advertising.

Words 2 Know!

You can also create your own mailing list. Ask people to sign up for **e-newsletters** by giving you their email addresses. Write an advertisement in an email and send it to everyone at once. You can include articles on your business, helpful tips, or trivia that might interest your customers. Only send e-newsletters to people who have given you their email addresses for that purpose.

Many businesses take online advertising further by using social media sites such as Facebook or Twitter. Social media helps you gain a following and spread the news about your products.

They even create **advergames**, which are games people play online whose characters, goals, **dialogue**, and **graphics** all promote the company and its products. When people play these games, they don't even know they're watching advertisements!

Do you like to watch movies? **Product placement** is when a specific brand, such as a can of Schweppes ginger ale, is visible on screen. You can do your own form of product placement. If you have a jewelry business, ask a friend to wear one of your necklaces to school or ask a parent to wear one to work. Give him or her the necklace for free along with a bunch of business cards to give to anyone who offers a compliment on the jewelry!

Dress For Success

While we all appreciate individuality, there are particular ways of dressing and behaving that are considered appropriate in certain situations. If you hope to convince investors to give you money for your business, you'll want to think about the appropriate way to dress for your presentation.

1 Match the nine characters shown above with one of the nine environments from the list below.

* wedding
* chorus concert
* skiing

* job interview
* rainy day
* picnic

* presentation
* school day
* beach

2 Ask a parent or grandparent to do the activity. Does he or she have different ideas about which outfits are appropriate to wear for certain events? Are there any outfits that could fit more than one setting?

Break a Bad Habit

Supplies: *paper, pencil, rubber band*

Imagine you're watching a business presentation and the entrepreneur is picking his ear or chewing his nails as he tries to tell you about his business! Luckily, any bad habit can be broken.

1 Write down whenever you do your bad habit. If you aren't aware of one, ask your friends—remember not to take what they say as an insult! Acknowledge whenever you do your bad habit and write down when it happens and what you think makes you do it. Maybe you bite your nails when you're nervous, meeting new people, or watching scary movies. You'll find a pattern in your behavior as you keep track of it.

2 After a few days of keeping track of your bad habit, replace it. Try wearing a rubber band around your wrist, and whenever you find yourself chewing your nails, snap the band against your wrist. This tells your brain that the behavior is a negative one and eventually the behavior will go away. You can also try simply taking deep breaths. By forcing your body to replace the bad behavior with a good one, you're training yourself to quit your habits.

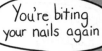

You're biting your nails again

Design Your Own Logo

Supplies: *magazines and newspapers you can cut up, scissors, 2 sheets of white paper, glue stick or tape, pencil, ruler, markers or colored pencils*

A logo is a symbol or simple picture that is an instant reminder to consumers of your business. Apple Computer's logo is the apple with a bite out of it. Coca-Cola uses a red can with a white wave to represent its soda. Logos are designed to catch consumers' attention and then to help them quickly recognize a business.

1 Look through some magazines or the newspaper and find five images of logos that you like. Cut them out and paste them onto a piece of paper.

2 Make notes about what you like under each logo. Why do you like them? Are they simple? Colorful? Do you like the **font** that is used in the text? Notice the combination of graphics and words.

font: type or characters that are all the same style and size.

Words **2** Know!

3 On another piece of paper, use a ruler to section the paper into a grid of eight equal boxes. In each box, make a sketch of a possible logo for your own business. In your first draft, don't add too much detail, just try to design the basic structure of the logo and the words you might use.

4 Don't expect to come up with the perfect logo the first time. Take time to consider your eight small drafts. Ask some friends or family members for their feedback. Choose the one you think is best.

Some colors have meaning associated with them. Red can mean energy or passion. Orange can represent modern thinking or innovation. Yellow can be sunny and optimistic, but can also remind people of caution signs on the road! Green is often used in connection with ideas about nature, freshness, or positive behavior. Blue is very popular and is often connected to professionalism and success, while purple shows creativity and imagination.

FUN FACT

Logo Guidelines

Keep these guidelines in mind as you create the logo for your businesses.

- **Remember what you are selling.** Figure out a simple way to represent what you're selling as a symbol or picture.

- **Think about your consumers or your audience.** If you are selling to kids, the style of your logo might be different than if you are selling to the elderly.

- **Keep it simple and bold.** Don't use more than two fonts for your text.

- **Think about color.** Choose colors that represent your idea. They should stand out. Using too many different colors can be confusing to consumers.

Advertise with a Stencil Printed T-Shirt

Supplies: *your logo or slogan, clear contact paper with one peel-off sticky side, craft knife, cutting mat, wooden board larger than your stencil area, white or light-colored plain cotton T-shirt (wash it first!), fabric or textile paint, small sponge roller, paint pan, clean white piece of cloth, iron*

What better way to advertise your business than to wear it around town? If you have designed a dynamic logo or if you've come up with a catchy slogan, use this technique to print it onto a T-shirt. Just by wearing your T-shirt you will be sharing your business with your community. Caution: Ask an adult to help with the craft knife and iron.

1 If your logo is simple, lay the contact paper on a work surface and use a craft knife to cut your design into it. If your design has details or letters, print it from the computer onto paper in black and white. Then staple your design to the back of the sheet of contact paper. Make sure the peel-off, sticky side is away from you and the clear, plastic side is facing up. Use the craft knife to cut out the design or letters in the contact paper. This will make a stencil of your design.

2 Place the board in between the layers of your T-shirt, under the area where you will print your design. Smooth the shirt to get rid of any wrinkles. Peel the backing off the contact paper stencil and stick the contact paper to your T-shirt.

3 Pour your paint in the paint pan. Work the roller in the pan until it is saturated with paint. Make sure there are no blobs!

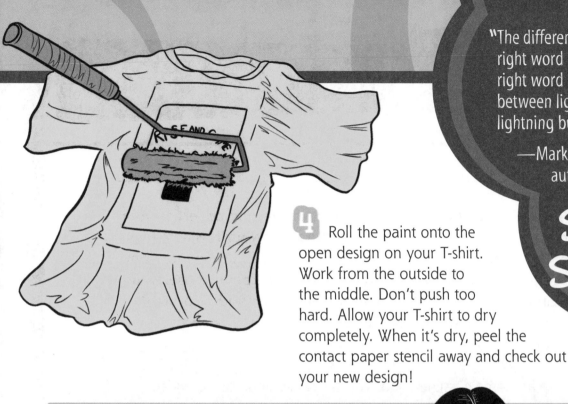

SAVVY SOURCE

4 Roll the paint onto the open design on your T-shirt. Work from the outside to the middle. Don't push too hard. Allow your T-shirt to dry completely. When it's dry, peel the contact paper stencil away and check out your new design!

5 Cover your dry design with the piece of white fabric or a piece of parchment paper, and iron over it to help the fabric paint stick permanently to the fabric. Make sure to iron over the entire area many times.

TRY IT: You can also use freezer paper to make your stencil. Print your image onto the regular paper side (not the glossy side). Cut out your design and then iron it with the glossy side down onto your shirt. The iron will fuse the paper to the shirt so it won't move when you apply the paint! Can you think of ways to use more than one color on your stencil design? Make more T-shirts for your friends and family! You can also print your design on other items to advertise your business.

Supplies: *phone or video camera, cooperative subjects for your video*

Video clips can be used in a number of ways to advertise your business or to help convince investors that your business idea is worth their money. Windows Movie Maker, iMovie, or Sony Vegas offer many editing tools and are all easy to use. You can also simply use a phone to make a clip and incorporate it directly into your business plan or on your web page.

1 Here are some possible things you could highlight in your video.

* **How your product is made** or how you provide your service. Imagine a sped-up video of you making the trash can alarm clock.

* **Profiles of you and your business partners.** Have everyone introduce themselves and explain how they will contribute to making the business work.

* **Customer reviews.** Interview a few people who use or have tried your product and record their comments.

* **Your company overview.** Video yourself explaining your company overview or the story you prepared in the activity, "Telling Your Story."

Create a Flyer

Supplies: *blank paper, colored pencils or pens, copy machine*

Small businesses post flyers around towns on bulletin boards or other public announcement locations. Flyers are papers with the business name and important information on them, and are an inexpensive way to spread the word about what you do.

1 When creating your flyer, include the important information about your business.

* Business name and logo.

* A short, clear description of what your business does. Use text from your company overview!

* Contact information—phone, website, and email address. Don't share your home address.

* Hours of operation.

* Pricing. How much will you charge for your product or service?

2 Organize your information around your new logo on one sheet of paper. Make sure that the font is big enough for everyone to read it, even if they are just passing by.

3 Make many copies of your flyer and post them around your town. Ask popular shops if they would be willing to post your flyer in their windows. Many banks have bulletin boards in their lobbies. Try to put up as many flyers as possible to get the word out!

Design a Website

Supplies: *computer with Internet access, pencil, paper*

One way to market your business is through a website. Your website can be as simple or complex as you want to make it! Web designers often start by drawing their websites on paper.

1 Always ask an adult before using the Internet. Look at other websites to get ideas. What makes you want to keep reading them? How do they organize information so that you understand what you're reading about? Is there anything you don't like about these websites? Remember to cover up neighboring QR codes to make sure you're scanning the right one!

2 Start designing your site on paper by sketching your homepage. This is the main page of your website. Add a header, which is like a title going across the top, and a few buttons to link to other pages, such as "About," "Products," and "Contact." Don't forget your logo!

3 Sketch the other pages on your website. What pictures will show your product best? Do you want to include a video?

TRY IT: Recreate your website on the Internet using a free website builder, such as one of the sites below. Remember to get your parents' permission and follow the Internet safety guidelines from page 76.

86

Chapter 5

Managing the Money

When starting a new business, you're going to spend lots of time thinking about money. How to make money, how to spend it, how not to lose it! Even the most passionate entrepreneurs realize that unless their new businesses make money, they're not going to be in business for very long.

Every business needs money before it starts making money. Does that sound strange? Where do you get money before you even sell your first item or perform your first service?

Some people use their own money to cover **startup costs**. This is money needed to buy supplies to make prototypes or purchase materials to perform market research and industry analysis. You might also need to spend money on marketing before you can start selling.

Words 2 Know!

startup costs: the money spent to start a business.

87

Remember Seth Priebatsch and his successful lemonade stand? He needed to buy more than just lemonade supplies to sell his product. Before he could start selling lemonade he needed money to obtain a selling permit and to build a lemonade stand.

You need to invest money into your business to make it work.

Some businesses need to pay rent for the space they work in or they need to pay employees or they need to buy equipment such as computers. Even people who start on a smaller scale need to think ahead and see the big picture. Remember one of the most important characteristics of an entrepreneur? Vision. Entrepreneurs plan for tomorrow.

Lots of new restaurants open every year.
But 90 percent of all restaurants that open in the United States fail in the first year.

FUN FACT

Investors

Savvy Source

"An investment in knowledge pays the best interest."

—Benjamin Franklin, American entrepreneur and inventor

One way entrepreneurs get the startup money they need is by attracting investors. Like entrepreneurs, investors are willing to take risks. They give money to new companies in the hope that the companies will become very successful and earn them more money than they invested. How does this happen?

You might have heard news stories about small businesses being bought by larger businesses. When this happens, the investors who first gave money to the entrepreneur get their money back, plus more depending on how much the business is sold for. As a part owner, an investor takes part of the profit.

Ideal Investor Timeline

Idea Presentation → Percent Agreement → Money Hand-Off → Company Thrives → Company Sells SOLD → Money Distributed

When investors make the original offer of money to an entrepreneur, they all agree on what percent of the company the investors own. That way there isn't any confusion later.

What happens if the company never gets sold? Maybe it will make enough money to operate on its own and pay the investors a return on their investments. Or maybe it will go out of business. An investor makes money if the business is successful and loses money if the business fails.

Why Do Investors Invest?

Every day, thousands of new businesses spring up all over the world. For investors, this means lots of opportunity to take financial risks that may pay off well.

How do investors decide which businesses to loan money to?

A few factors go into an investor's decision. First, the investor considers the entrepreneur starting the business. Is she passionate about her idea? Is she hardworking? Does she show an eagerness to learn and a willingness to ask for help if she needs it? Can she manage her time well?

Investors want to be sure that their money will be used by someone qualified to run this particular business. Remember your executive summary from chapter 2? Investors will pay close attention to the part where you describe your unique qualifications for this job.

Investors want to make a profit from the money they invest.

The second factor investors consider is your product. Can you convince investors that your product or service is something people will want to buy? Is it useful? Is there a need for it? Does it make the world a better place?

Investors will also be interested in how much money your business will make. Of course, we all plan on making lots of money with our new businesses, but investors will want to look at real **expectations** based on planning. They want to see numbers!

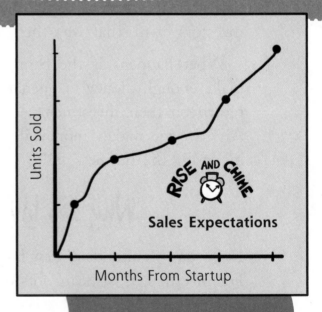

Sales Expectations

Units Sold

Months From Startup

expectation: a belief about what might happen in the future.

Words 2 Know!

Buy the Best

American investor Warren Buffet is well known for his brilliant investments. He once said, "It's far better to buy a wonderful company at a fair price than a fair company at a wonderful price." What does he mean? If a company is doing an okay job and it only costs $5 per share, do you think this is a better investment than a company doing a great job that costs $10 per share? Why? Remember, a share is a tiny piece of the company that an investor can buy.

donor: a person who gives money to an individual or organization with no expectation of anything in return.

mission: the goal of a person or organization.

Words 2 Know!

Investors give money away for other reasons, too. Many nonprofit businesses are supported by a special kind of investor, called a **donor**, who gives money with no expectation of getting paid back. They donate money because they believe in the **mission** of the nonprofit. They understand that the community will be improved by the work of the nonprofit and they are willing to spend money to see that work accomplished.

Loans and Credit Cards

Another option for getting the money you need for your business is to find someone to give you a loan. Friends and family members are possible sources for loans.

Many new companies do not get loans when they are first starting up. Can you think of why? Adults usually get their loans from banks, and banks prefer to avoid risks. Plus, loans must be paid back, usually with monthly **installments** that include interest over the course of a few years. Do you think a new business will find it easy to make those payments?

Words 2 Know!

installment: a regular payment of a debt.

Be prepared to present your business plan to anyone you ask for a loan, just as you would to an investor.

As a kid, you might find that a friend or family member will be willing to wait a while before being paid back the money he or she loans you. Maybe your aunt will say yes if you ask to borrow money, and will agree to wait one year for you to repay it.

92

Your aunt wants you to succeed and agrees to loan you money. But she also wants you to learn from the experience of starting a business and she might require that you pay interest on the loan. Say she's going to loan you $100 to cover your startup costs. At a 5 percent rate of interest, you will pay her back that $100 plus 5 percent. How much will you owe her at the end of the year?

Numbers 2 Know

What is 5 percent of $100?

The word percent means per 100, or out of 100. As a fraction, we write this as 5/100. We say "five out of one hundred" or "five per one hundred." Imagine coloring in five boxes in a 100-box grid. You colored 5 percent of the grid.

5 percent interest of $100 = $5 interest

Do your parents have a credit card? They might use it to buy groceries or pay for vacations. Credit cards allow people to buy something without paying money for it right away. Instead, they agree to pay back the money, plus interest, on a monthly basis.

Credit cards are very convenient, but they can also be hard to manage. Some people pay off only a little bit every month even though they keep buying things. Soon they owe the bank thousands of dollars. Sometimes an entrepreneur uses a credit card when he or she is first starting a new business. This is a huge risk. If the business fails, the entrepreneur still owes the money he or she charged to the credit card, even though the business didn't make any money.

The very first credit cards were made of paper and had a $300 limit.

FUN FACT

Microcredit Makes a Big Difference

For adults living in the United States, $27 is not a lot of money, especially when you're trying to start a business. But for a group of people living in India, $27 made a huge difference. Muhammad Yunus, a social entrepreneur and banker, loaned that exact amount of money to a group of 42 women living in poverty in the Indian village of Jobra. The women wanted to start a business making bamboo furniture. They used the loan to establish a successful business and paid back the money plus interest.

Yunus called this kind of lending **microcredit** because the amounts of money were very small. In 1983, he established the Grameen Bank, which means "Village Bank," to lend small amounts of money to groups of people. Group members help each other start businesses and pay off their loans. The Grameen Bank still does this important work, and Yunus even won a Nobel Peace Prize for his efforts. This is one of the highest honors in the world.

Muhammad Yunus
Nobel Laureate

microcredit: a loan of a very small amount of money.

Words 2 Know!

Pricing

How much are you going to charge your customers for your product or service? You may be tempted to just name a price, but first you need to do some research.

Your price is a careful balance between your expenses and what people are willing to pay.

Consider how much money people will be willing to pay for a trash can alarm clock. You've already done some research about what other companies charge for their alarm clocks and how well those alarm clocks sell, so you have some guidelines for pricing your own product.

If you know that alarm clocks that cost more than $20 do not sell well at the stores you visited, you might not want to charge $22 for your alarm clock. But if you make a really great alarm clock, will people be willing to pay more? This is one of the business decisions you will have to make.

Many entrepreneurs take little or no money in the beginning. This can help a business grow.

If you find that your expenses and time cost more than what you can expect people to pay for your product, you'll have to do some thinking. Can you save any money on expenses? Maybe you can buy some of your materials in **bulk**, which will be cheaper. Can you save any time? If you make your alarm clocks on an assembly line rather than one by one, it will make the process go faster. Are you willing to make less money per hour?

bulk: buying lots of the same product at the same time, which is usually less expensive per unit than buying in smaller amounts.

Words 2 Know!

Projections

Once you figure out how much your product or service will be sold for, you can make financial projections about how much money your business will make.

Let's revisit the trash can alarm clock example. Your market research shows that 50 percent of the 1,000 families in your town have children who need to be awake by 7 a.m. five days a week. This is your market. How many of those families will buy your trash can alarm clock? Say you can sell a trash can alarm clock to half of your market:

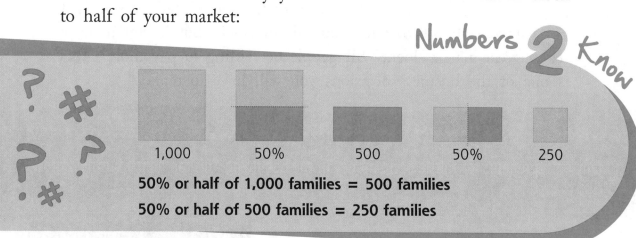

Numbers 2 Know

| 1,000 | 50% | 500 | 50% | 250 |

50% or half of 1,000 families = 500 families
50% or half of 500 families = 250 families

Because you kept careful records, you know that it costs you $5 in materials and two hours in time to make one trash can alarm clock. Say you want to charge $5 an hour for your time and another $3 per item for your profit:

Numbers 2 Know

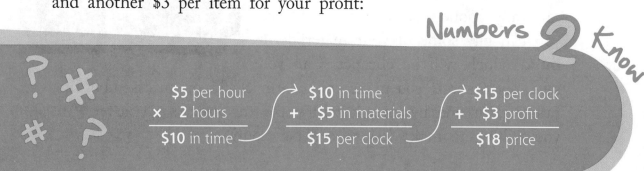

	$5 per hour		$10 in time		$15 per clock
×	2 hours	+	$5 in materials	+	$3 profit
	$10 in time		$15 per clock		$18 price

There are more expenses to consider. You know that each alarm clock costs $15 to make. Maybe you spent another $100 on marketing. What is your **net income**?

Numbers 2 Know

250 alarm clocks
× $18 each
———————————
$4,500 Total Income

250 alarm clocks
× $15 to make
———————————
$3,750 Total Cost

$100 Marketing Expenses

$4,500 − $3,750 − $100 = $650 Total Profit (Net Income)

These projections also work if your business provides a service instead of a product. Let's say your new business is walking dogs. You can ride your bike to your client's house, and you walk the dog for half an hour. It takes 15 minutes to ride your bike each way. If you want to make $5 an hour, how much do you need to charge?

Service businesses are a little different than selling products. Imagine you had a repeat customer who paid you to walk her dog every day during the week. Let's say you'd earn $5 times five days, or $25 every week. Some businesses find that the guarantee of income makes it worth lowering the price a little bit. You might charge $5 to walk a dog once a week, $4.75 per day to walk the dog three days a week, and $4.50 per day to walk the dog five days of the week.

Repeat customers are important to a business. They allow you to spend less on marketing.

FUN FACT

97

Sales Plan

Supplies: *pencil, paper*

You've done a lot of hard work to prepare your business for success. Now it's time to put a plan in place for actually selling your product or service!

1 Brainstorm different actions to sell your product. Actions to get your product into the hands of customers are different from the marketing strategies explained in chapter 4.

2 Make a chart with a column for action, pros, and cons. Pros are the reasons for something. Cons are reasons against something.

3 Under action, write each of your sales ideas. Under pros, write the good things about that idea. Under cons, write the bad things about that idea.

ACTION	PROS	CONS
Set up a sales table at the local farmers market.	The market is right down the street from your house. The market is always crowded when you go there.	$25 table fee. You'll have to stay at the market for four hours. You'll need to bring a table and chair.
Ask a local storeowner to stock your product	You won't have to spend time selling your product. People will see your product when they come to buy other things.	The storeowner might say no to your request. The store gets a percentage of your profit.

4 Choose two actions to try. Will you choose the actions with the most pros or the fewest cons? Maybe one action has some cons, but you try it anyway. Entrepreneurs sometimes choose the option that most people would avoid.

5 For the two actions you choose, make a list of next steps. These are things you need to do to put your action in motion. If you choose to ask a local storeowner to stock your product, your list might start like this.

* **Decide on which store to ask.** Think about the contacts you made during your market research.

* **Write a letter to the storeowner** explaining why people will want to buy your product. Use some of your marketing language. Also include how much money you need to make from each sale and how many units you can supply in the beginning.

6 Start selling! Beginning with your first next step, perform your list of things to do for each action. If your first two choices don't work out, move on to the next two. Keep trying until you are selling your product on a regular basis.

TRY THIS: Keep track of all of your communications and results. If you ask a storeowner and she says no, you don't want to ask again by mistake!

Natural Disaster

One thing business people have no control over is the weather. Bad storms can have a huge impact on a business's ability to survive. A business that has the bad luck of getting battered by a hurricane stands a good chance of failing. When Hurricane Sandy hit the coastal town Red Hook, in New York, in 2012, dozens of businesses were flooded. Some business owners had insurance that gave them the money to rebuild, but many owners didn't have enough money to rebuild and reopen. Business people who'd spent years building their companies saw their work simply swept out into the ocean.

99

Budget in Excel

Supplies: *computer, Excel spreadsheet software*

Spreadsheets are like super calculators. You can write equations that compute what you need to know about different numbers typed into different cells, so you don't have to redo your math every time you make a change in your costs. In this activity, you'll learn how to use a spreadsheet to keep track of your expenses so you can make a budget.

Words 2 Know!

cells: the blocks in a spreadsheet where data is entered.

1 Open a new Excel spreadsheet. The icon looks like the letter "X". Every column has a letter and every row has a number. Each cell is named with a combination of these letters and numbers: A1, B3, C2, and so on.

	A	B	C	D	E
1	**A1**	**B1**	**C1**	**D1**	**E1**
2	**A2**	**B2**	**C2**	**D2**	**E2**
3	**A3**	**B3**	**C3**	**D3**	**E3**

Cell
← Column
← Row

2 To put a number in a cell, click on the cell, type the number, and press enter. To delete a number, click on the cell, press delete, and press enter. Your numbers appear in the cells and also in the input line above your columns next to this symbol: f_x. If you create a formula in a cell, the formula will show up in this spot as well. Practice inputting, deleting, and replacing numbers.

f_x	= B2*C2

← Input Line

3 Delete your practice numbers and type a series of random numbers in cells B2, B3, B4, B5, and B6. If you added them up, how much would it be? Across the top of the spreadsheet are several headings, such as "Home," "Layout," and "Tables." Click on "Formulas." Now click on cell B7, the cell just below your list of numbers. Look near the top of the spreadsheet for a symbol such as this Σ with the word "AutoSum" below it. Click on it and press enter. You have created your first formula for adding up numbers in a column.

	A	B
1		
2		2
3		4
4		10
5		8
6		9
7		=SUM(B2:B6)

4 Now make this into the start of a budget. Let's say you need five different items to make a trash can alarm clock. Label column A "Cost of Goods Sold" and list your five materials underneath. Change the numbers in column B to the price of each material. What happens to the number in cell B7 when you are done? This is your cost of goods sold.

	A	B
1	Cost of Goods Sold	
2	Material 1	2
3	Material 2	4
4	Material 3	10
5	Material 4	8
6	Material 5	9
7	Total	33

5 One way to learn how to use Excel is to experiment with it. Can you figure out how to change the numbers into dollars and cents? Can you find out how to highlight different rows or columns?

TAKE IT FURTHER: To complete your **budget**, make new spreadsheets for marketing expenses and sales expenses. Try to include everything!

Words 2 Know!

budget: a plan for how money will be spent.

Financial Projections

Supplies: *computer, Excel spreadsheet software*

Once you know what your profit will be, you can predict your revenue—the amount of money you might be able to make in the future. Spreadsheets are helpful for this!

1 Let's calculate what you should charge for your product. On a new spreadsheet, label your columns with the titles used in the example below.

	A	B	C	D	E	F
1	**Materials** cost per unit	**Labor Hours** per unit	**Hourly Wage**	**Labor Cost** B x C	**Unit Cost** A + D	**Price to Charge**
2						
3						
4						

2 You know that the cost of materials for each alarm clock is $5, so type 5 into cell A2. It took you two hours to make each alarm clock, so type 2 into cell B2. You've decided you'd like to earn $5 per hour. Type 5 into cell C2. You can format the numbers to be Currency or General.

	A	B	C	D	E	F
1	**Materials** cost per unit	**Labor Hours** per unit	**Hourly Wage**	**Labor Cost** B x C	**Unit Cost** A + D	**Price to Charge**
2	5	2	5			

Words 2 Know!

revenue: money made by a business from selling products or services.

3 Now tell the computer what to do with your numbers by creating a formula. You can use the Formula Builder or type in your formula manually.

Formula Builder:

* Click on cell D2, then go to "Formulas" and click the "Formula Builder" button.

* Scroll down the list and double click "Add, Subtract, Multiply or Divide." Select "*(Multiply)" from the operation toggle list. Cell D2 is now: =*

* Click on cell B2 on the spreadsheet. Cell D2 is now: =B2*

* Click on cell C2. Cell D2 is now: =B2*C2

* Press enter.

Manual Formula:

* Click on cell D2 and type "=" on your keyboard.

* Click on cell B2. Cell D2 is now: =B2

* Type "*" (shift 8), this is the symbol for multiply. Cell D2 is now: =B2*

* Click on cell C2. Cell D2 is now: =B2*C2

* Press enter.

You've created a formula to calculate your "Labor Cost" for the alarm clock.

	A	B	C	D	E	F
1	**Materials** cost per unit	**Labor Hours** per unit	**Hourly Wage**	**Labor Cost** B x C	**Unit Cost** A + D	**Price to Charge**
2	$5	2	$5	=B2*C2		

4 Use what you learned in step 3 to create a formula for the "Unit Cost" in cell E2. You want to add Materials cost per unit (A2) to Labor Cost (D2).

5 The last column is the price you will charge for one alarm clock. To make money, this must be higher than your Unit Cost (E2). Choose a profit amount, such as $3 per unit. Write a formula in cell F2 to add $3 to the Unit Cost.

Chapter 6

Where the Future Begins

Congratulations! You've done lots of hard work to prepare for the start of your new business and you deserve to feel proud. Even as your business starts to make money and support itself, there is still a lot to do. You need to keep organized records of all the work you, your partners, and your employees do. How can you continue to make your product better? Can you improve your marketing strategies to attract more customers? Are there other products or services that would be a good fit for your company? Where do you go from here?

We've talked a lot about why entrepreneurs succeed. You need to be passionate about your idea, willing to work hard, and be able to ask for help. You need to have grit and be willing to learn from your mistakes. Plus, your idea needs to be something people will pay money for. And you need to launch at the right time.

You're in the Money

You've learned about setting prices, attracting investors, and keeping track of your business expenses and income. You need to pay this same kind of attention to the money you have earned. Knowing how to handle your money is called **financial literacy**, and it's an important skill for every business owner.

Words 2 Know!

financial literacy: understanding how money works in the world.

reinvest: to put profits back into a business.

stock market: a market where shares of companies, or stocks, are bought and sold.

Successful businesses are the result of hard work, a lot of luck, and financial smarts.

As you make more money, you might feel tempted to spend more. Maybe there's a skateboard you've had your eye on or maybe you want the newest generation iPod. Before you lay down your hard-earned cash to purchase something you want, consider your options. Could you **reinvest** your money into your business? Is there a charity that you believe in? Maybe you will need that money in the future and it makes sense to keep it safe in a savings account. Or you can put your money to work for you by investing it in the **stock market** and hoping it grows during many years.

Reinvest

Many entrepreneurs decide to wait a while before receiving paychecks from their companies. This is another example of taking a risk in the expectation of a larger reward in the future.

If you decide not to pay yourself the $10 to build every trash can alarm clock you sell, that's 10 more dollars that can go toward materials, advertising, and other marketing. That's $10 you don't have to borrow. That $10 may turn into $20 or $30 when your business is more successful. By not taking a paycheck today, you may be earning a greater paycheck tomorrow.

If the business does not succeed, you've lost that money. Again, it's a risk you choose to take.

Save

You've probably heard of savings accounts. Maybe your parents already have one set up for you. Savings accounts are where you put the money you decide not to spend. Your money will earn interest in a savings account at a certain rate.

Savings accounts don't earn a high interest rate, but they do make it easier to save money. If you don't have the cash, you're less likely to spend it. Savings accounts also allow you to withdraw your money whenever you want.

Saving is an important practice for both kids and adults. Life can be expensive—cars, houses, college, vacations, and retirement all cost a lot of money. If you can start saving when you're young, it will be much easier to face big expenses later. Even if it sounds boring, putting money into savings is a very wise choice.

Words 2 Know!

compounding interest: interest paid on both the initial amount of money plus whatever other money has already been earned in interest.

Compounding Interest

Saving money can seem like magic with **compounding interest**. It works like this: You earn interest on money you leave in a bank account, right? When that interest stays in the account, it also earns interest. And then that interest earns interest. And so on and so on.

Would you rather have $10,000 or a penny a day doubled for 30 days? Most people say $10,000, because that's a lot of money, and who knows what doubling a penny every day will get you. But it turns out that if you double your pennies every day, after a month you'll have $10 million! No bank offers a doubling interest rate, but this shows how much money you can get even when you start with just a little bit.

Numbers 2 Know

Day	Total Number of Pennies
1	1 penny or **1¢**
2	3 pennies or 1¢ × 2 + 1 = **3¢**
3	7 pennies or 3¢ × 2 + 1 = **7¢**
4	15 pennies or 7¢ × 2 + 1 = **15¢**
30	1,073,741,823 pennies or **$10,737,418.23**

If you put $100 into a savings account that earns 0.75 percent compounding interest, and you deposit $10 every month, after 10 years you'll have $1,353.53.

Other ways of saving money include putting it into a **certificate of deposit (CD)** or investing it in the stock market. Usually you get higher interest rates with these methods. However, these types of investments have restrictions and risks.

A CD pays a higher interest rate, but it requires you to leave your money untouched for a period of time, anywhere from one month to five years. If you save your money in a CD and you need some money right away to buy supplies for your business, you can't take it out without paying the bank a penalty.

When you invest your money in the stock market, you take the risk that the companies whose stock you buy might not do well—you could lose your money. In addition, most financial advisors suggest that you invest in the stock market for a long period of time. It is not a good way to save if you plan to take money out all the time. Your decision of which method to use to save your money will depend on how much time you have and how much risk you are willing to take.

certificate of deposit (CD): a written notice that a bank will hold a customer's money for a certain amount of time and pay interest on it.

Words **2** Know!

Financial advisors call the amount of time you plan on leaving your money in an investment account or in the stock market your "time horizon."

FUN FACT

108

Give Back

Why would you give away your hard-earned money? That sounds like a strange way to practice good financial habits!

You learned earlier that some people invest their money in charitable organizations. These donors can be corporations or individuals. They donate money to different charities depending on what their passions are. This way, they help to make their communities and the world a better place.

Are you crazy about animals? Check out the local humane society. Do you feel terrible that some people have no homes and have to sleep in parks? See if there's a homeless shelter in your town. Do you think every child deserves an education? There may be a nonprofit organization in your area that supports that passion. Nonprofits are able to help others because of people like you who share a passion for their causes and choose to help with financial donations.

"Wealth is not to feed our egos, but to feed the hungry and to help people help themselves."

—Andrew Carnegie, American businessman and philanthropist

Savvy Source

Business Bio: Bill and Melinda Gates

The Bill and Melinda Gates Foundation is one of the largest private foundations in the world. Bill Gates, founder of Microsoft, has promised to give away half of his enormous wealth over the course of time. He and his wife believe that part of the responsibility of having a lot of money is sharing with those who need it. They have chosen to focus on extreme poverty, healthcare, education, and access to technology. Melinda Gates says, "The premise of this foundation is that one life on this planet is no more valuable than the next."

What's Next?

The future may feel like it's far away, but the truth is it always comes faster than you expect. You may have started your business thinking that you'd own it forever. Or maybe you just wanted a fun way to make some money while you're in school. Or you're hoping to sell it and move on to your next entrepreneurial adventure.

> Whatever your expectations are, it's a good idea to keep them in mind as you continue to establish and grow your business.

Successful new businesses often try to find buyers to purchase their companies. Or, if they are really good at what they're doing, buyers will approach them. You may have heard stories on the news of small companies being bought for millions of dollars by larger companies. These are rare success stories. The people who started those small companies worked hard and also got very lucky. But never be discouraged from pursuing this kind of result.

Individuals, corporations, and foundations in the United States donated about $298 billion to nonprofits in 2011.

FUN FACT

Entrepreneurship is a fascinating combination of work, luck, and inspiration. Whatever your plans for the future, the work you have done as an entrepreneur will serve you well. Creativity, ingenuity, and persistence are all traits valued by teachers and people who might hire you when you're older. The skills you've learned in this book will make you a better student, employee, or boss. What does the future hold for you?

The activities in this book have led you step by step through the process of creating a business plan. Now you can put it all together and create one comprehensive plan for your business. This plan will change as your business grows, and you may need to add sections later on. You'll want to reread it every couple of months to update the information. But it's a good foundation for your first business.

Words 2 Know!

compile: to gather.

1 When you present a business plan to a possible investor or share it with someone you are hoping might give you advice, you'll want to have it look clean, organized, and professional. Take time to **compile** the work you have completed while doing the activities in this book into a final business plan that you can share. Your business plan should include the following items.

* **Cover:** Include your business name and logo, your name, and the names of your partners.

* **Company Overview**

* **Executive Summary**

* **Industry Analysis**

* **Market Research**

* **Marketing and Sales Plans:** Include your logo and design process, as well as your flyer and any other advertising.

* **Financials:** Include your spreadsheets showing your budgets, projected expenses, and income, as well as your plans for saving, giving, and spending.

* **Funding Sources:** List your investors if they have given you permission to use their names.

111

Interviewing Entrepreneurs

How can you learn more about being a successful entrepreneur and get feedback about your ideas at the same time? Ask questions of those who have come before you! Every community has many successful business people, and most of them will be willing to share their experiences with an interested young person—you. All you have to do is ask in a professional, thoughtful manner.

1 Start by asking your parents and friends about local entrepreneurs. Make a list of three people who started their own businesses who you would like to interview.

2 Look at your time management calendar and talk to your parents to find at least three times you are available to meet.

3 Call or email your entrepreneurs. Plan what you are going to say before you dial the phone! Explain who you are and why you would like to talk with them. Ask if they are willing to meet and what times are good for them.

4 Prepare! Write down a series of questions you would like to ask the entrepreneurs. Ask about his company, its history, how he manages it, and his successes and struggles. You'll find that your questions will depend on your own experience and your own business idea. Don't be afraid to ask for advice! Also, have your business plan organized and ready to share.

5 Conduct your interview! Remember to dress appropriately and arrive a few minutes early. Pay attention to your body language, just as if you were giving a presentation to a potential investor. Plan to spend about half an hour interviewing your subject. Bring a recorder to record the interview, and write notes during the interview as well. You don't have to write down every word your subject says, but a few key words will help you remember the important parts.

6 Don't forget to mail a thank-you note!

Business Bio: Nick Woodman

Nick Woodman loves to surf. When the first business he started failed, he decided to travel and visit some of the world's best surfing spots. To catch himself catching the waves, he used a small camera strapped to his wrist with rubber bands. Aha! That gave him the idea to make cameras that people could attach to their clothing, equipment, or helmet to capture great action shots. He and his girlfriend sold shell necklaces out of their van to raise money to start GoPro, which is now worth more than $2 billion.

Part of GoPro's marketing strategy is to spend millions of dollars a year to have the GoPro name linked through social media to photos of both amateurs and professionals doing amazing things on skis, surfboards, mountain bikes, skateboards—anything adventurous. When Felix Baumgartner broke the world record by jumping out of a plane from 24 miles above the earth, he was wearing five GoPros.

113

Supplies: *3 jars of similar size, labels, markers, large rubber band*

Savvy entrepreneurs not only save money for the future and invest in their own businesses, they also give back to their communities. Having a savings bank with three different compartments will allow you to know just how much you have saved, how much you can spend, and how much you are able to give away.

1 Label the three jars "Save," "Give," and "Spend." Connect them using the large rubber band.

2 Decide which charity to support. You'll make the greatest impact if you choose one charity and give to it for a long time instead of spreading your donations out over different charities.

3 Create a savings plan. For example, every time you earn $5, $3 goes in Save, $1 in Spend, and $1 in Give. Even though saving feels difficult right now, it is the most important part of financial literacy. Always put the biggest portion of your money into the Save jar.

4 Every month, take the money in Save and deposit it in your savings account at the bank. Bring the money from Give to the charity of your choice. Finally, spend the money in Spend on something you want for yourself or reinvest it in your business! New entrepreneurs usually put off buying personal items so they can reinvest in their companies to make them stronger. But once in a while, treat yourself to some fun with your hard-earned money.

Glossary

advergame: an online game that attracts players to certain products without their knowledge.

advertise: to attract attention to a product, service, or business.

assembly line: an arrangement of workers and tasks in a line that make assembling products faster.

attain: to achieve something.

barter: to trade one item for another item.

BCE: put after a date, BCE stands for Before Common Era and counts down to zero. CE stands for Common Era and counts up from zero. The year this book is published is 2014 CE.

brainstorm: to think creatively and without judgment, often in a group of people.

budget: a plan for how money will be spent.

bulk: buying lots of the same product at the same time, which is usually less expensive per unit than buying in smaller amounts.

business: the act of making, buying, or selling goods or services in exchange for money.

business plan: a written plan that describes how a new business will reach its goals.

cells: the blocks in a spreadsheet where data is entered.

census: an official count of the people living in a country.

certificate of deposit (CD): a written notice that a bank will hold a customer's money for a certain amount of time and pay interest on it.

characteristic: a feature of a person, place, or thing.

charitable foundation: an organization that raises and donates money to a specific cause.

chief executive officer (CEO): the highest-ranking person in charge of a company.

collaborative: working together with other people.

colonize: to take control of an area and the people who live there.

communicate: to share information in some way.

community: a group of people who live in the same area.

competition: an event at which different teams or individuals compete against each other for an award. Also, a person or company or group that you are trying to succeed against.

competitive: when someone is trying to do something better than other people.

compile: to gather.

compounding interest: interest paid on both the initial amount of money plus whatever other money has already been earned in interest.

concise: giving a lot of information in only a few sentences.

consumer: a buyer of goods or services.

creative: using imagination to come up with new ideas or things.

credit: paying for something later or over time.

Glossary

currency: money or other valuable item used for exchange.

customer: someone who buys goods or services from a business.

data: information, facts, and numbers.

demand: the amount that people want to buy.

demographic: a group of people that shares the same qualities, such as age or gender.

dialogue: conversation between characters in a book, movie, or video game.

document: a written record of something.

donor: a person who gives money to an individual or organization with no expectation of anything in return.

draft: an early version of a piece of writing, which will be revised.

durable: lasting a long time.

earbud: a small headphone that fits in the ear.

efficient: wasting as little time or effort as possible when completing a task.

e-newsletter: an email newsletter.

engineer: someone who uses science, math, and creativity to design and build things.

entrepreneur: a person who takes a risk to start and operate a business.

entrepreneurship: taking a risk to start a new business.

equipment: the things you need for a certain activity.

establish: to set up on a permanent basis.

expectation: a belief about what might happen in the future.

expense: the amount of money needed to pay for or buy something.

facial: having to do with the face.

fee: an amount of money paid for a service.

feedback: helpful information or criticism given to improve something.

financial: having to do with money.

financial literacy: understanding how money works in the world.

financial projections: the prediction of a company's future expenses and profit.

financial report: an official record of the financial activities of a business or organization.

font: type or characters that are all the same style and size.

forage: to collect food in the wild.

founder: the person who starts a business.

founding: the group of people that starts a business.

fund: to pay for.

generate: to create something.

global: all over the world.

goods: things for sale or to use.

graphics: pictures and animation.

guideline: a general rule.

habit: a regular behavior that is hard to give up.

Glossary

hesitant: slow to act or speak.

incandescent: containing a wire that glows when heated by an electric current.

increment: a small part of something bigger.

industry: the large-scale production of something.

industry analysis: the collection of information about other businesses in a market.

innovation: a new invention or way of doing something.

inspiration: having great ideas.

installment: a regular payment of a debt.

instant camera: a camera that prints the photograph immediately after it's taken.

interaction: the action or influence of people, groups, or things on one another.

interest: the fee charged for the use of money in a loan.

international: happening in more than one country.

inventor: a person who makes something new.

invent: to be the first to think of or make something new.

investor: a person who agrees to give time or money to an enterprise.

jingle: a short song used in advertising.

key player: a person who will help you start your business.

keywords: the subject words in a sentence or phrase.

letterhead: a sheet of stationery printed with the name, address, and logo of a company.

listserv: an electronic mailing list.

loan: money that is borrowed and paid back with interest.

logo: a symbol used to identify a company that appears on its products and in its marketing.

low-income: describes a group of people who don't earn enough money to meet basic needs such as food and housing.

market: an opportunity for selling, either in an area or to a particular group of people. Also, to advertise or promote a product or service.

marketing: communicating in different ways to make a business known.

market research: the collection of information about people who may become customers.

meditation: spending time in quiet thought.

mentor: a person who advises and guides a younger person.

merchant: someone who sells something.

microcredit: a loan of a very small amount of money.

miller: someone who grinds wheat into flour.

mission: the goal of a person or organization.

Glossary

monetary system: the system used by a country to provide money and to control the exchange of money.

monopolize: to take over and completely control something.

motion study: finding the most efficient way of performing a job.

motivating: giving someone a reason to do something.

mutiny: a revolt or rebellion against authority.

net income: a company's earnings after expenses are paid, also known as profit.

netiquette: rules of appropriate behavior for the Internet.

nonprofit business: an organization focused on improving a community in some way. It relies on donations to pay its costs.

nonverbal communication: behavior that sends messages without spoken words.

obligation: something that must be done.

Oceania: a large group of islands in the South Pacific.

opportunity: a chance to do something.

option: a choice.

packaging: the wrapper or container that holds a product.

partner: a person who shares the work and reward of a business.

passionate: having strong feelings about something.

permit: an official document that allows you to do something.

persistent: refusing to give up or quit.

personality: the characteristics and ways of behaving that make people different from each other.

PowerPoint: a computer program used for making slide-show presentations.

presentation: an activity in which someone shows, describes, or explains something to a group of people.

press release: an official announcement sent to newspapers or magazines.

product: an item, such as a book or clothing, that is made and sold to people.

productive: working hard and getting good results.

product placement: putting products in movies or television shows as a form of advertising.

profit: the money made by a business after all expenses have been paid.

prototype: a first or early model of something new.

qualification: a skill or experience that makes someone suited to a particular job.

quantity: the number or amount of something.

recreation program: a program designed to encourage people to have fun and relax.

recruit: to get someone to join you or help you.

reduce: to use less of something.

regulation: an official rule or law.

reinvest: to put profits back into a business.

resourceful: able to deal with new or difficult situations and to find solutions to problems.

revenue: money made by a business from selling products or services.

risk: the chance that something bad will happen.

savings account: a bank account for saving money.

scientific management: the management of a business to increase efficiency.

service: work done by one person for another person.

share: a small part of a business that can be sold for money.

shareholder: someone who owns shares of a business.

slogan: a phrase used by a business or other group to get attention.

social entrepreneur: an entrepreneur who identifies and works to solve social problems to bring about sweeping, long-term change.

social media: websites where people can write messages to each other.

solution: an answer to a problem.

spreadsheet: an interactive document on the computer that computes and keeps track of numbers.

startup costs: the money spent to start a business.

stock market: a market where shares of companies, or stocks, are bought and sold.

survey: a series of questions asked to gather information.

tax: money charged by a government.

technology: tools, methods, and systems used to solve a problem or do work.

trade route: a route used to carry goods from one place to be sold in another.

transportation: a way of moving people and things.

vision: an idea of what we want in the future.

web page: a digital document found on the World Wide Web.

website: a group of web pages on the Internet that all relate to one business.

wireless: a device that can work without wires.

BOOKS

Kidpreneurs: Young Entrepreneurs with Big Ideas. Adam Toren and Matthew Toren. Business Plus Media Group, LLC, 2009

Growing Money: A Complete Investing Guide for Kids. Gail Karlitz and Debbie Honig. Price Stern Sloane, 2010

Better Than a Lemonade Stand! Small Business Ideas for Kids. Daryl Bernstein. Aladdin/Beyond Words, 2012

WEBSITES

Junior Achievement: An organization that offers classes for grades K-12 on entrepreneurship and financial literacy.
juniorachievement.org

Biz Kids: Videos, games, and lesson plans about financial literacy
bizkids.com

All Terrain Brain: Music videos, games, and an activity guide about entrepreneurship
allterrainbrain.org/ATBHome.aspx

QR CODE GLOSSARY

Page 51
moma.org/explore/multimedia/videos/122/709

Page 54
census.gov
factfinder2.census.gov/faces/nav/jsf/pages/index.xhtml

Page 66
mathsisfun.com/data/graphs-index.html
nces.ed.gov/nceskids/createagraph/default.aspx
jmathpage.com/JIMSStatisticspage.html

Page 86

Example Websites
kids.nationalgeographic.com
pigeonandpigeonette.com
noodoll.com
brainpop.com

Free Website Builders
education.weebly.com
lifeyo.com
snappages.com
doodlekit.com

Index

Index